OUT OF DARKNESS
Stories from India

OUT OF DARKNESS
V.G. HARLEY

WORD PUBLISHING

Word (UK) Ltd
Milton Keynes, England

WORD AUSTRALIA
Heathmont, Victoria, Australia
SUNDAY SCHOOL CENTRE WHOLESALE
Salt River, South Africa
ALBY COMMERCIAL ENTERPRISES PTE LTD
Balmoral Road, Singapore
CONCORDE DISTRIBUTORS LTD
Havelock North, New Zealand
CROSS (HK) CO
Hong Kong

OUT OF DARKNESS: STORIES FROM INDIA

Copyright © 1988 Word (UK) Ltd

ISBN 0-85009-103-9

Typesetting by Suripace Ltd, Milton Keynes.
Reproduced, printed and bound in Great Britain for Word (UK) Ltd by
Cox and Wyman Ltd, Reading.

With grateful thanks to D., our dear friend

Gateway to India
BOMBAY

OUT OF DARKNESS

Stories from India

GLOSSARY OF INDIAN TERMS

Rupee	Unit of Indian currency: equivalent to less than 5p.
Paise	One hundred paisas equal one rupee
Puja	Hindu worship ceremony
Mantra	Hindu text used in incantation
Bottu	Hindu caste-mark worn by women on the forehead
Caste	Hindu division of class, with *Brahmins* as the highest caste.

Brahmins were originally the priests and scholars. These still hold most of the influential positions in India today. There are also levels of Brahmins.

Kshatriyas represent the 'warrior class'. Previously these were the kings, soldiers and warriors. Now many of this caste are landowners and large-scale farmers. The third caste level is *Vaishyas* or traders. The fourth level is *Sudras*, now craftsmen and small landowners.

Harijans, formerly 'untouchables' are sometimes villagers, sometimes illiterate, and sometimes do menial and degrading jobs. Some now succeed in leaving the villages and, with an education and perhaps a clerical job, are less easily definable in caste structure.

Gunja	Hashish - a drug
Sadhu	Holy man
Standard	Education level like a form or grade: children study to twelfth standard (sixth form)
Lunghi	Men's wraparound trousers
Karma	The Hindu and Buddhist belief in one's fate or inevitable consequence.
Bhagavad Gita	(or 'Gita') a famous poem within the Hindu Scriptures.

INTRODUCTION: THE GOD WHO FLED

"Wouldn't you like to visit the ashram?" one of my hosts asked, eager to please. It was my first visit to India, and there was so much to see.

"No thank you!" I shuddered. Already I had heard about the orgies and violence in the 'Bhagwan's' enclave on the other side of Pune, and I had seen Westerners drifting down the Lakshmi Road in their orange robes and Rajneesh medallions. It was definitely not on my 'must see' list.

At the church we visited the following Sunday, the text was from the Book of Judges, and the story about Gideon: the least in his father's house, but chosen to lead a rag-tag army and defeat an enemy as big as a nightmare. An evening or two later, whilst sitting on the wide porch at the Guest House, I thought again of Gideon. And then it seemed that God was drawing my attention to the ashram not far away. What did it mean?

The answer came through prayer: God would use a band of spiritual warriors throughout the land to bring new blessing to India. The prayers of many ordinary Indian Christians would join together in new power. *And these prayers would also be effective in dispelling evil from that ashram!*

"But how, Lord?" I wanted to know. And how was I involved in all this? He didn't answer that one, so I simply prayed on. It was hard to have faith - to believe on such a scale. And where were the others in "Gideon's army"? But God *had* spoken. So I kept praying.

I left Pune the following month and flew home to England. For ten weeks the story of Gideon, the ashram and God's promise were constantly in my thoughts. One night in a Manchester hotel, I had a vision: I was standing at the base of a mountain just outside Pune, when suddenly a huge rock was dislodged from the top of the mountain and came hurtling down the side. God impressed these words upon me:

> *If you say unto this mountain,*
> *"Be removed," and doubt not.....*

Seven nights later, BBC Television broadcast a special report: THE GOD WHO FLED. Rajneesh had left the ashram, Pune and India.

But who, I kept wondering, were those other 'Gideon's warriors' throughout India who believed that faith can and does move mountains? Subsequent visits were to provide some wonderful answers.

ONE

Good news for India

*Thou hast made me known to friends
whom I knew not. Thou hast given me
seats in homes not my own. Thou hast
brought the distant near and made a
brother of the stranger.*

Rabrindrath Tagore.
Gitanjali

The streets of Bombay, the Gateway to India, were alive with noises and movement. My well-worn Ambassador taxi dodged its way through a thousand other Ambassadors, rickshaws, oxcarts, bicycles and jostling humanity. Not for nothing is this city known as the 'Melting Pot of India'. From high-rise offices to cardboard shacks, from business-suits and brightly coloured silk saris to the khaki shirts of the destitute beggars crowded on the pavements, Bombay reflects all the diversity and confusion of India today, a mixture of desperate poverty and eastern riches. On earlier visits I had taken home silk carpets, ivory beads or an inlaid box... but this time I was looking for treasures of a different kind. I had come to find and meet some of the present day disciples of Jesus Christ living sacrificial lives of faith and service in hidden corners throughout India.

The car clattered through some old green gates in the Nana Chowk area and I found myself in a compound surrounded by balconied buildings, once a Mission School, now bleached by more than a century of sun. I was greeted by a tall, sandy-bearded man who led me upstairs into a shaded room filled with plants and books, the decor a happy mixture of East and West. But then Ray Eicher himself is a similar mixture...

Born in India to English parents then adopted by American missionaries, he has lived in India most of his life. His Indian passport affirms he's an Indian - he just looks a bit different from most of his countrymen! Today he is one of the two co-ordinators of the work of Operation Mobilisation (OM) in India. With colleague Alfy Franks his task is to train Christian young people first to love and serve God and second to love and serve their fellow man. They oversee some thirty-five teams operating from six centres around India. Several thousand OM'ers share the love of Jesus in cities, towns and villages throughout that vast land.

But what directed Ray's steps to this work with OM? While studying medicine at Taylor University in the USA in the early 1960's, Ray attended a prayer meeting which was addressed by the founder of OM, George Verwer. He challenged the students to 'go into the world and preach the Good News of Jesus Christ'. He stirred them to a militant faith that would lead to prayer for the world, that would see lives changed, that would believe God for accomplishing the impossible. Ray sensed that this meeting was the turning point in his life. He said to God, "Here I am: whatever You want to do with me, it's OK". Afterwards Ray told George Verwer of his total commitment to Jesus Christ and that he was willing to place his career before the Lord. George Verwer made the surprising response: "Go back to India".

In 1964 the first OM team arrived in India. Ray joined them and soon developed a love for literature that has never left him. He tells a story typical of those early years:

"An OM team was in Bihar in 1968. The trucks stopped on the main road and the team climbed out to give literature in their own language to the local people. Two small boys reached up for their free tracts. They read them carefully and then noticed an address where they could write for a free Bible correspondence course. The boys did so, and soon received their first lesson. They enjoyed their studies so much that they told their friends about them. Soon other correspondence courses were ordered. A little class began to grow in the village. And yet there was no church there, no ongoing Christian witness.

"Today the village has a church with Christian families, a Christian school and Christian pupils. The two boys joined

OM teams for training and are now at college for further preparation."

At one time Ray found himself getting very depressed, feeling overwhelmed and even guilty that there were so many unreached by the good news of Jesus. "God showed me something from that," Ray confided. "He said I'm not responsible for those I can't reach: I'm only responsible for those I can. Giving out pieces of Christian literature to everyone within arm's length is how I can do it!" So these days Ray never leaves the OM compound without his wallet of tracts and Scripture portions in each of the fourteen major Indian languages. When he sits on a bus, he can't resist asking the person beside him where he's from. In a moment Ray has pulled out his bulging wallet and the surprised stranger is offered a gift booklet in his native tongue.

Among the young people training with OM in Bombay is a pretty Hindu-born Bengali girl. Now in her mid-twenties, Mina is waiting for the right time to return to West Bengal to work for Jesus there...

It all started when Mina began to share her troubles with her friend Sephaly. She always felt reassured when she talked to Sephaly, who was like an aunt to her, though she had troubles enough of her own. Her mother-in-law practised witchcraft in an effort to harm Sephaly when she discovered she was a Christian. Sephaly's husband was a Communist and he too was angry with her beliefs, regularly restricting her movements. Mina noticed, however, that her friend's difficulties seemed less important to her than the love she felt for Jesus.

"Always take your burdens to the Lord," Sephaly advised her, "He is the way and the truth and the life." At first Mina didn't understand how someone you couldn't see could make such a difference to your life. Sephaly never even had an image of this Jesus! She never brought food to Him on the shelf. But she often prayed to Him, and some days she even went without food herself and devoted the meal-time to praying in her room.

"No man comes to God except through Jesus," Sephaly explained gently to her young friend. Mina's parents said prayers to many gods, but Sephaly was different. To Mina's parents, coming before the god-shelf was just another daily duty and it didn't seem to make them any happier. When people did things they didn't like they got very angry, whereas Sephaly would just smile and go off and talk to Jesus about it.

Before long Mina began to think about Jesus for herself. She discovered that He had healed many sick people, and even brought some back to life. In two ways, He was different from anyone else who ever lived: when murdered He came back to life again, and shortly afterwards was seen to disappear in the clouds. At that time His followers heard Him promise: "I'm going to be with you always, even to the ends of the earth." But the most wonderful thing about Jesus was that even though He was the only man who never sinned, He was willing to be punished for the sins of the world! Mina could hardly believe this at first. Why would He do such a thing?

"Because God loves everyone," Sephaly explained, "He wants to be their Father, and be with them always." Mina longed for such a loving Father. These days her step-mother caused her much grief and her father did not try to understand. Mina often wanted to stop her Hindu prayers, her *mantras* and *pujas*, but her parents always made sure she kept up the ceremonies. Often she'd have to take the gods off their shelf and wash them, and she'd say to herself, "These are just pieces of wood and plaster. They're not gods at all. I can't pray to them anymore!"

One day Mina was invited to spend a few days with a Christian couple. They showed her much love and taught her many things about Jesus. But then while living with her sister's family she became ill with typhoid, came close to death and for three or four months was too weak to eat or move. Alone on her cot she thought much about the stories of Jesus she had heard from Sephaly and the couple she had visited. It was painful to think how Christ had suffered at the hands of cruel men, being falsely accused and executed even though He had done no wrong. What a waste of His perfect life.

But Sephaly used to say that it wasn't wasted. She often reminded Mina that if Jesus hadn't died for us we'd have to bear our own punishment for our sins. And then we'd never know God as a loving personal Father! Mina thought of Christ's suffering and compared it to her own. She wasn't going through her troubles to give life to even one person, but Jesus endured horrific pain *because He loved everyone*. All the stories she heard and the words she read came with full force into her heart. She especially remembered one:

> That if you confess with your mouth Jesus
> is Lord and believe in your heart that God
> raised Him from the dead, you will be
> saved.
>
> (Romans 10:9)

Mina believed with all her heart that God had raised Jesus from the dead! But she had never told anyone this. Suddenly she felt she would burst if she didn't speak of Him! She sat up on her cot and said aloud: "Oh yes, Lord, I do want someone like You who will be with me always. Someone I can open myself to and can trust completely. I know I've been a sinner and I'm so sorry for all I've done. I want to put my love and life in Your hands." She sat there quietly, feeling that the rest of the world had dropped away and only Jesus was there with her. Her heart absolutely bubbled when she thought of Jesus. Because even though she had just chosen Him, in a way too wonderful for words, she felt that He had chosen her!

The doctor had recently told her that she needed six months more of bed rest, much good food and vitamins before she'd return to normal. Suddenly Mina knew that something had happened to her body, too, and that the doctor was in for a surprise!

The very next day she got up and dressed, and began to tell her friends and family about Jesus' love. From then on, each day brought new strength. A lovely old man began to visit Mina and pray with her.

"Wouldn't you like to serve the Lord Jesus?" he asked her.

"How can I?" Mina replied, feeling downcast. "I have no proper knowledge to serve Him!"

The man told Mina about Operation Mobilisation and how it trained young people like herself to be Christian workers. He promised to go home and pray about this, and Mina began to pray too. She soon realised that something in her heart was telling her that was what God wanted. Mina wrote to OM in that first year as a new Christian and was overjoyed when they finally accepted her for training.

For six years Mina wrote letters to her father, but he never replied. Then out of the blue she received a letter in his handwriting! When she opened it up, her face fell. It was a demand to renounce her beliefs and her friends and come home. He spoke of all the Hindu gods and goddesses. "Are they all lies?" he wanted to know. "The Gita: is that all lies? And what is your duty to us who gave you birth?" He reminded her of a Bengali verse in which the poet said,

> The whole world may leave me but I will
> do my duty.

"You say you have Jesus in your life and yet you left us! You say you have happiness. How can you be happy killing someone?"

It was obvious that her father was not interested in her opinions. She also suspected why he was asking her to come home. As a girl of marriageable age, she could be kept there against her will and married off to a non-Christian man.

She looked hard at the letter again, and her eyes fell on the verse of poetry:

> The whole world may leave me but I will
> do my duty.

When Jesus was alive He went here or there and paused before various men who were busy at their work. Gently He told them, "Leave that: come and follow Me." And that's what they did. *They did their duty.* Mina knew that even though she would be misunderstood, criticised and perhaps even hated, she had to do her duty to the One who had not flinched from His duty to save her.

"I want to go home again," she told me, " but I am waiting to see what God tells me to do. I'm sure I shall return to West Bengal someday; I want to work for Jesus there. But God will show me when to go back...."

My heart was linked to Mina, and to those other young people in OM who turned out to be part of the 'Gideon's army' God had shown me on my first visit. Little did I know, when I began praying about the ashram, that they had the same burden. One day they prayed, I heard later from Ray Eicher, that Rajneesh's voice would be stilled. Exactly one week later the 'Bhagwan', following his hasty departure from India, took a vow of silence which lasted almost four years.

TWO

"He called me brother!"

Here is thy footstool and there rest thy feet where live the poorest, and lowliest, and lost.

Rabrindrath Tagore
Gitanjali

Jacob Sengodan comes from the village of Attayampatti in the Salem district of Tamil Nadu. Fifteen years ago, a quarter of the village moved to Bombay. A severe drought had ruined their meagre crops, and the mechanisation of the handloom industry on which they were dependent created increasing hardship for many families.

Jacob's mother and sister moved to Bombay first, and then they sent for him. It was time for Jacob to make a new start. As a young man with limited prospects, he had got caught up in the world of liquor smuggling. At first he would make only four rupees a day, but eventually he was making twenty rupees a time. He learnt to move by night, transporting liquor from one village to another. Coming from a hill tribe surrounded by forests, he was able to get about without being detected. He became the ideal person to graduate to gunja smuggling.

The work was hard. Jacob carried many pounds of gunja more than a hundred miles over difficult and dangerous terrain. Sometimes his trips would take eight or ten days. Even so, he earned barely enough to support himself, his wife and daughter.

Three times he was caught, arrested and imprisoned. The first time he was jailed for three months. The last time he was given a six month sentence and put in with hardened criminals. He saw many suffer from harsh treatment and insufficient food. Men died because of beatings from the warders or violence from other prisoners. Jacob wondered whether he would come out alive, and considered himself lucky when he was released. He returned to the only work he knew, carrying gunja. By this time he was drinking heavily and addicted to the drug. It meant he had even less to live on.

When his mother moved to Bombay and then sent for him and his family, he thought it might give them a better chance. Bombay did not quite live up to his expectations. It was true that there were big buildings and luxurious cars, but you could not touch these things from the pavement.

Jacob began picking up rags to sell to the paper works. He would also collect and sell glass. And it seemed that his life rose no higher than the pavement where he lived and worked.

One day he found a leaflet printed in Tamil. It gave a Tamil address but then something else was printed in English, which Jacob could not understand. He held on to the paper and kept working, always looking here and there for the smallest scrap of value. He stopped to watch a crowd form round a young man who was talking - no, he was preaching. Jacob thought of the Danish mission school which he had briefly attended as a boy. He recalled the lady missionary who had spoken about Jesus Christ, and how it had struck a chord in his young heart. He'd even promised to follow Jesus, and the missionary had prayed with him...

Now as he came closer, the young preacher was talking about Jesus too. He was saying that He loved us so much that He died for our sins, so that we could be forgiven. Jacob looked at the paper in his hand and thought perhaps this young preacher could tell him what was written in English. When he had finished speaking, Jacob went up to him. The well-dressed man turned and saw Jacob, very dirty and wearing a soiled shirt and lunghi. He put his arm around Jacob and said, "How are you, brother?"

At that moment something crumbled within Jacob, something that had been hard and brittle for many years. He found tears rolling down his cheeks and a dirty hand quickly wiped them away. The preacher translated the words on the leaflet, which offered a correspondence course. Jacob could barely utter "Thank you" before stumbling off.

He kept thinking: *He called me brother!*

Thirty year old Prabhu Rayan couldn't forget that encounter either. As he boarded the bus that afternoon to return to his home some distance from the slum area, he felt God saying to him, "You called him brother! If he really were your brother, how many times would you have visited him?"

It was a rebuke to him and Prabhu knew what he must do. Before that time he'd felt God leading him to go and preach in the slums. Was God now saying he should do more than that?

The next day Prabhu returned to the slum and found out where Jacob slept. He found him with his wife, under a plastic and rag covered shelter. Jacob's wife was nine months pregnant and they were both full of fear. Little by little Prabhu learned about their lives and misfortunes. Jacob had one older daughter but his wife had been unable to bear children for many years. She had finally had a baby, but he was born with a hole in his head and died soon afterwards. Jacob and his wife were terrified that this child too would be malformed and die. Prabhu laid his hands on Jacob and his wife, and prayed that God would give them a perfect baby. He asked God to bless the family and show them how much He loved them.

That afternoon Prabhu preached to the people again. This time he used the Bible story of Hannah, who cried out to God for a child, and promised to give him back to God to serve Him. When Samuel was born, she kept her promise. Most of the people listened for a time, then drifted away. But Jacob didn't miss a word. Something was happening in his heart that he couldn't explain.

Three days after Prabhu prayed, Jacob's wife gave birth to a healthy boy. They called him Samuel. Jacob looked down at that perfect little body and wondered whether God was saying something to him about a new life. After all the fear and pain and suffering, a new life had been given them. Perhaps it could be like that for Jacob.

When Prabhu returned, he read them something from the Bible:

> Therefore if any man be in Christ, he is a
> new creature: old things are passed away,
> and behold, all things are become new.
>
> (2 Cor. 5:17)

Jacob received that verse with great joy. God had spoken to him! That was his first day as a *new creature in Christ*. From then on Jacob became a friend of Prabhu and his wife Nancy, and it was in their home that I heard his story. He still lives in the slums, and is known as one who prays for the sick and has seen people healed.

Prabhu had been called by God to work in the slums in 1979. One day he invited all the pavement children for a picnic. He took them on a bus to a park and bought them sweets. Afterwards as they were sitting on the grass, Prabhu told them a story and then taught them a chorus:

> Yes God is good
> Yes God is good
> Yes He's so good
> He's so good to me!

One little girl of nine who had been very sick had such a wonderful time at the picnic that she kept singing the chorus at home. One day she climbed up on her mother's lap and sang again:

> Yes God is good
> Yes God is good

and suddenly she vomited, and died. It was found later that her intestines had been badly twisted by worms. Prabhu was shocked at the news. He went immediately to the little slum shelter to share the parents' grief. He sat with them in silence for a long time, and finally said, "Your child cannot come back to you but there is a chance that you can go to your child. Wouldn't you like to consider that way?"

And he told the mother of the Heavenly Father who

loved the world so much that He allowed His Son to come to earth to take the punishment for our sins. Prabhu invited the grieving mother to accept Jesus into her life and she did so!

There was a leper lingering by the doorway, and rats scurrying round the shelter. There were soiled rags on the floor, but Prabhu didn't notice these things until the mother said, "Brother! You can eat now!" and she brought out some dishes and put them before him. Prabhu had never been put in a situation like this before! His first thought was, "Oh no, I can't..."

He hadn't been brought up that way; he was not used to that sort of life, having enjoyed a relatively protected upbringing. After school he had studied plastic technology in Madras, intending to do further study in the West. He came to Bombay before going abroad, working in a factory to save some money, and stayed with a doctor in his comfortable home. Of course one couldn't live in Bombay for a day without seeing poverty spilling out at every other corner. He saw these things, certainly; but it wasn't part of his life. He never *felt* them...

Then one day in 1979 a friend took Prabhu to a slum. It shocked and devastated him but at the same time he felt God saying something to him:

> Every place that the sole of your foot shall
> tread upon, that have I given unto you, as I
> said to Moses.

"What could that mean?" Prabhu kept wondering. As he prayed and listened, it became clear to him: he was to walk among the slum people, claiming God's blessing for them, sharing the good news of Jesus with them, and God would redeem the lives of many.

Prabhu looked at the enormity of the problem. In Koliwada alone there was prostitution and criminal activity of every description. But then he looked to God, and knew that what God orders, He also supplies. If He was pointing

Prabhu in this direction, He would also equip him for the job.

Prabhu left his work in the factory and within a few days was back in the slum. On the first day he found two Christian families and brought them together for a prayer meeting.

The first person to feel the impact of Christ's love was the wife of a criminal. For the first time in her life, she felt God speaking to her and knew she must accept Jesus Christ. Later her husband, who had spent six years in prison, became a believer. After that a slumlord's son was converted. Soon there were five new Christians, faithfully studying the Bible and anxious to be baptised.

All these things flashed before Prabhu as he sat there in that miserable hut: amidst the squalour, yet among new friends who were offering what little they had.

"I just can't," he thought again desperately.

Then God whispered: *"Obey me, that I may be glorified"*. Prabhu reached out to take the food from the woman, and began to eat. The next Sunday, as he preached again in the slum, ten people responded to the appeal and committed their lives to Christ.

Prabhu began to think of marriage. It was time he found a wife, and he began to pray for God's guidance. At the same time, he thought, "Who on earth would be willing to share my work in the slums?"

He answered his own question: "Any girl willing to sit in the midst of these people and eat and drink with them, will be the one!"

Eighteen year old Nancy Sam sat in the church next to her girlfriends during the Good Friday service. The preacher was speaking from Romans 3:23: "For *all* have sinned, and come short of the glory of God....." Well that certainly didn't apply to her, she thought with a toss of her head. She was a well-brought-up Christian girl, whose father did much evangelistic work in the Methodist Church. There was strict Christian discipline in their home, with daily Bible reading and regular church going. Of course she never went to the cinema, and of course she was a Christian! "For all have sinned, and come short of the glory of God." He was saying it again, more forcibly than before. Nancy shifted in her seat, resentment closing in. "Anyone would think he was addressing *me*," she complained silently. She thought of her college classmates, Hindus, Muslims, going to the cinema, mingling with the opposite sex, drinking, smoking. She always felt different; she was not at all like them!

"....We can sin through pride, in thinking ourselves better than others...." Nancy was shocked when she heard that, but shock wrestled with indignation, and the latter seemed to be winning.

"....or we can sin through anger, refusing to accept what God says about us...." That was when her defences began to crumble. It was no use arguing with God. Somehow all the verses she'd learned over the years drifted back now, reminding her that "You must be born again". Belonging to a Christian family was not enough. Jesus had said to Nicodemus, a good religious person, that one had to be born *spiritually, born again by God's Spirit*, in order to make personal contact with God. How many times she'd heard that! And only now did it make sense.

That Good Friday was a red-letter day for her. She humbly acknowledged to God that she was a sinner. What's more, she went to the front when the preacher made an appeal, and publicly professed Jesus Christ as her Lord that night.

Nancy completed her B.A. in 1972 but later that year was devastated when her mother died suddenly. It meant looking after her younger sister and brothers in the midst of her own great grief. For weeks she moved about mechanically, doing her chores, caring for the family, but without the joy in life she once knew. One day she recalled something her mother had said before she died: "I'll be very happy if you'll be a missionary some day. I don't desire success for you, but I do want you to serve the Lord."

Nancy began to compare this period of listlessness and mourning with her mother's aspirations for her. "Why have I had all this training?" she wondered. "What am I doing with it?"

"We'll have a party," she suddenly announced to her surprised family. It was nearing Christmas and Nancy thought of the thirty to forty children in the building where they lived. She'd get them together for a Good News Club and teach them about Jesus again. It had been too long since she'd thought about those youngsters.

Nancy studied for an M.A. and was also assistant editor for a pharmaceutical magazine. But she couldn't shake off the conviction that she should teach. Eventually she returned to college for teacher training and obtained her B.Ed. Her family wanted her to marry. There were some good proposals over the years. A few men had secular jobs; some were working abroad. None of these offers seemed right to her. The Lord seemed to be saying, "Why do you worry about getting married?"

Later she and a girlfriend locked themselves in a room and prayed in earnest: "Marriage or no marriage, we are for You, Lord! We dedicate our lives to You...."

One day in 1980 Nancy went to a Marathi church to help with some Bible studies. Some friends said, "There's a Tamil boy who sometimes comes here. Would you like to meet him?"

Nancy thought her father might say she'd just come to meet the boy. "No," she told her friends. "No thanks."

One of her friends, a rather insistent one, said, "His name is Prabhu..."

Strangely enough, not long afterwards an uncle told her father about a Tamil boy of the same name who attended the Bombay Christian Centre. Her father said, "OK, let's meet him."

The uncle told Nancy: "He's from the Bakht Singh group of Brethren, so he'll believe in adult baptism. You'd better get baptised that way!"

Nancy retorted: "I'll not get baptised again to get any man!"

She admitted to herself that this was a baffling issue. She

had been 'sprinkled' as an infant in the Methodist Church, and as a teacher in their Sunday School she didn't think it would be right to go against this teaching. On the other hand she noticed that in the church she attended, their own pastor didn't sprinkle his own infant, but preferred to have a simple dedication ceremony instead.

She couldn't help feeling that a Christian ought to make the decision for himself. "After all," she reasoned, "salvation isn't something you get from your parents. You have to take that step of faith yourself."

Even so, she didn't want to do anything to embarrass her father or make him unhappy.

The issue was decided a few days later as she was reading 1 Peter 3:21:

> The like figure whereunto even baptism doth also now save us - not the putting away of the filth of the flesh but *the answer of a good conscience toward God....*

Nancy heard from a friend about Prabhu's work. She thought to herself, "If he really works in the slum, I want to see this."

One Sunday she took the bus to the Vile Parle area where Jacob and his family lived, and asked to be directed to the place where meetings were held. She entered the hut and saw people sitting round on the earth floor, waiting for the service to begin. Nancy thought of a chorus, and decided to teach it to them while they waited. She sat down in the middle of them and began to sing. Just then Prabhu entered the hut, looked at her, and rushed out again. "What a strange fellow," Nancy thought to herself, "rushing out like that." And she continued to teach them the song.

Prabhu had to run from the tent because he was so overcome. As soon as he saw her sitting there, he knew God had brought him his wife. And he had to rush out to thank Him.

THREE

Those who sit in darkness

*I shall be wise this time
and wait in the dark, spreading my mat on
the floor; and whenever it is
thy pleasure, my lord, come silently
and take thy seat here*

Rabrindrath Tagore
Gitanjali

Prabhu and Nancy were married on July 4, 1980. A few months after the wedding, Prabhu's widowed sister began to visit them daily. And every time she came she'd say, "Why don't you do something about the blind people?"

Prabhu was busier each month with his preaching - both in the slums and in the churches where he hoped to create interest in the slum work. After all, it wasn't enough to go to the slum-dwellers and tell them of Christ's love. They had to be able to go to a local church and be part of the Christian community. It wouldn't do to have a 'slum church' because other Christians didn't accept them into the 'normal' structure!

Many a time he earnestly prayed: "Lord! I didn't give birth to a child just to see it die!" It was not an easy road to travel. Prabhu had to admit that all Christians weren't welcoming the slum-dwellers with open arms. Some were very hesitant about it, to say the least. Prabhu thought regretfully of his own attitude in the past. Once he had even beaten a boy with a shoe because he'd fallen in love with a girl from a higher caste. And more recently hadn't it crossed his mind to take up the good carpet so as not to soil it when the slum-dwellers came for a visit? If he could entertain such thoughts, could he be so hard on other Christians for feeling the same? So there was much work to be done - on both sides.

And then there was Prabhu's sister, day after day, saying,

"When are you going to do something about the blind people?"

It was toward the end of 1981 when Prabhu had to go away for some weeks of meetings. Nancy was on her own with their five-month-old daughter when someone asked her to take a message to a blind lady. She had never been in a blind person's home before, and was surprised to find the little hut clean, neat and tidy. She had always thought that blind people were beggars! That was her first surprise.

A few days later her daughter came down with an infection and became very ill. Her temperature kept climbing and Nancy feared the worst. She prepared to take the baby to hospital. Just then a blind man arrived at the home. He'd heard that the baby was ill, and offered to go for medicine and food.

For the next few days first one then another blind person came to visit and to give Nancy a hand. She was quite overcome at what they could do and how lovingly they helped her. As the baby responded to the medication the Lord seemed to remind Nancy: "They have been more faithful than your relatives or your closest friends."

When Prabhu returned, they prayed about what God wanted them to do, and a few days later they were reading from the prophet Isaiah:

> I, the Lord, have called you in righteousness; I
> will take hold of your hand. I will keep you and
> will make you to be a covenant for the people
> and a light for the Gentiles, to open eyes that
> are blind, to free captives from prison and to
> release from the dungeon those who sit in
> darkness.
>
> (Isaiah 42: 6,7)

"How can we give sight to the blind?" they asked the Lord. And the answer came: "We can be eyes for them when needed. We can give them help and hope to lighten their darkness."

Shortly afterwards a blind youth named Param came into

their lives as 1981 was drawing to a close. It had been *The Year of the Handicapped*. He was born Paramasivam in Bombay, twenty-nine years earlier, although his family came from the Salem district of Tamil Nadu. When he was in the Seventh Standard he had begun to lose his eyesight after an illness, and in six months he was totally blind. His parents, in great distress, took him to many temples, offering gifts and doing *pujas* to implore the gods to restore his sight. But nothing happened.

Then, because they heard that *neem* leaves are sometimes used to remove devils, they took the leaves and squeezed out the juice into his eyes. When that didn't help, they took rust and rubbed that in.

It was a terrible thing to be blind, but it was equally terrible to have a blind person in the family. Many considered it a bad omen, a stigma. Often a blind person would be hidden away to that others could not see the family's shame. Now these same attitudes kept Param doubly in darkness. And for six years he spent most of the time indoors.

"I have lost the most precious thing in life," he cried day after day. He often went without food, so heart-broken was he. In 1976 he went to the hospital on his own, determined to find out what could be done.

"I'm afraid it's too late now," the doctor told him with regret. "We could have operated and reversed your original condition, but the substances put in your eyes destroyed the nerves around them. I'm afraid we can do nothing now."

After that Param made a real effort to come to terms with his disability. "Now I know I'm always going to be blind," he told himself, "I shall have to accept it." He was still grieving, and still frustrated, but at last he was starting to think about his future: a future that included blindness. He remembered when as a boy of twelve or thirteen he used to help an old blind couple and went shopping for them. Incredibly, the couple heard about his situation, although it had been a carefully guarded secret, and came to visit him! Before long they began to teach him Braille. Param began to venture out now, and one day he stopped on a corner where he heard a crowd gathering and someone speaking.

The man was speaking about love: the love of God. Paramasavam should have known all about that: his name meant 'the love of Shiva'. He smiled to himself. "If that's the case," he wondered, "why is Shiva always pictured with a spear in his hand?"

> Herein is love, not that we loved God, but that He loved us, and sent His Son to be the substitute for our sins. Beloved, if God so loved us, we also ought to love one another.
>
> (1 John 4:10-11)

"What kind of love is this?" Param asked himself, feeling something new stirring in his heart. "I want to know more about it," he decided then and there.

When Prabhu was preaching he saw the young man with expressionless eyes standing apart from the others, listening attentively. When he finished he went over to Param and spoke to him. "Whenever you wish to come to my home," Prabhu said finally, "you will be most welcome!"

Param returned to his hut with growing excitement. The next morning he awoke with the same joy and desire to hear more about this love of God. He would go to the preacher's house as he suggested! Prabhu and Nancy had found a house a short distance away in an area Param knew when he was sighted. So it wasn't difficult to make his way there that morning. He opened the gate, walked slowly up the steps and knocked at the door. Nancy came out and saw the stranger standing on the porch. He had red eyes and was staring strangely. "Perhaps he's on drugs," she thought anxiously; "perhaps he's a thief." "My husband's not here!" she said sharply, her tone telling him to move along. Then she went indoors.

Param turned away from the house and retraced his steps along the lane. Never had he felt so rejected and frustrated! He had thought, hoped and believed he would be welcome, but yet again he had been turned away. With these thoughts he went back to his hut.

In a moment Prabhu rushed in, out of breath. "I'm sorry, my friend," he explained apologetically, "I forgot to tell my wife you were coming! Unknowingly, she turned you away." He put his hand on Param's shoulder, inviting him to return. They walked back to the house, deep in conversation. Almost at once Param said, "I want to hear more about Jesus Christ."

That morning Prabhu showed him the way to reach God. He explained that although God loves the world, mankind's sin separates him from a holy God. What bridges this gap? Jesus - who willingly 'paid the price' for our sins:

> Greater love hath no man than this, that a
> man lays down his life for his friends.
>
> (John 15:13)

Prabhu showed him that all we have to do is to trust Jesus Christ as the only Saviour and way to God:

> For as many as received Him to them gave He
> the power to become sons of God even to
> them that believe in His name.
>
> (John 1:12)

Param didn't need any time to think about this. He decided at once that this was *for him*. He had found the secret to life itself!

"There is someone who loves me," he wanted to shout for joy. "I have a reason for living." Memories of sorrow and misery dropped away, never to return. He told his friends: "Jesus Christ came to save and help me. I can now depend on Him to do everything for me!"

Param was a regular visitor to Prabhu's home after that, eagerly studying the Bible. When he heard that there were Tamil services held in a Methodist Church in Bombay, he eagerly learnt the way and began to attend. He was baptised a Christian just a few days before Christmas 1981, and this is when he took the name Paramanaldam, meaning *joy all the time*.

Events moved swiftly for him now. He was interviewed for a railway job, selected and put on a waiting list. Then a Christian engineer learnt of an opening in a factory and he was offered that job too. After so many years of idleness, the thought of a good job was attractive. But Param thought of all the blind people in double darkness as he had been. He became convinced that God was calling him to a new work of leading others to Christ.

When Prabhu suggested a meeting for them, Param gathered ninety-five people and led them to Prabhu's house! That was the beginning of a new vision for Param.

Prabhu, meanwhile, has gone on to work with the India Fellowship for the Visually Handicapped, through which he arranges camps for the blind and sighted, organises fellowship meetings and maintains Braille libraries. But he's also involved in linking blind people with local churches, enlisting volunteers and conducting seminars for workers. His aim is to run fourteen camps a year, one in each of the major languages.

"God doesn't want the blind isolated," Prabhu told me. "They must be integrated into society, and into the Body of Christ. That's why we like our camps to have an equal share of sighted and handicapped."

About a dozen Bombay churches play a part in the blind work, but Prabhu would like to see more getting involved. "With a hundred thousand blind people in Bombay alone," he said, "it's a problem Christians can't ignore. That's one in every seventy. And there are nine million throughout India."

On my way back to my flat near Chowpatty Beach I saw a slogan scrawled on a wall:

UNTOUCHABILITY-
A CRIME AGAINST GOD AND MAN

It was a privilege to have met Prabhu and Nancy, and see how they were unceremoniously tackling this problem - in Jesus' name.

FOUR

On the waterfront

*Ascribe to the Lord
the glory due to His name;
Worship the Lord in the
splendour of His holiness.*

Psalm 29:2

One Monday morning I was on my way to Bombay's Mazagon Docks, India's largest dockyard. Elsewhere throughout the country you see activity and inactivity woven together in a uniquely Indian cloth. Here, passing through heavily guarded gates, it is all work and bustle: lorries, cars and men moving purposefully and urgently beside the docks.

The car lunged toward the main building scattering all around it. Suddenly guards were everywhere, snapping to attention. I was whisked out and up into a fine old building full of polished wood. The Victorian lift took me to the top floor, to a door which read V. FRANKLIN, GENERAL MANAGER.

Once inside I waited anxiously with his henchmen for the awesome presence to appear, but I needn't have worried: Victor Franklin was all friendliness, modesty and good humour. Clearly effective in managing four thousand employees, he was at the same time a soft-spoken Christian gentleman who did not spare himself to welcome me and assist me in meeting other friends and colleagues whose lives had been changed by Jesus Christ.

Victor comes from Andhra Pradesh, one of seven children of a Christian headmaster. His parents both worked in a missionary school and hospital, but it was not until he was a young sailor in Bombay that Victor took the step of enlisting in the active service of Jesus Christ. He saw that a religion was of little use to the second generation if one didn't have a personal experience of one's own.

Now many years later, Victor looks back on a long and interesting career. "Each day brings its problems," he told me, "but it is wonderful to know the wisdom of the Lord Jesus and the peace and joy of having His Spirit within me."

One unique aspect of the life at Mazagon Docks is a prayer meeting in which Victor's colleagues and workmen come together to pray through business problems or personal needs. That morning as we talked, some of these colleagues came in, and Victor introduced them to me. One young man named Sam, a Marine Surveyor at Mazagon, was from a Christian family. Another, a Mechanical Engineer named Murty, was originally a Hindu who first heard about Christ whilst a student in college. Coming from very different backgrounds, both men reached a point when they chose personally to follow Jesus. They saw this as essentially an individual decision, regardless of parental beliefs held or family traditions practised.

Victor made a suggestion: would I like to meet a naval officer named Mishra, formerly a Brahmin priest? He was stationed some distance from Bombay, but agreed to receive us at his home the following night.

We tore along in the darkness, our Le Mans driver heedless of potholes, ditches, ox-carts or any other moving thing. For most of the journey my attention was - mercifully - diverted from the road by the young doctor seated next to me, who came along for the ride... or perhaps to tend possible casualties! Dr Stephen Alfred, M.S. is a general surgeon who qualified in Bombay and is now a Senior Registrar in a government hospital. His own spiritual pilgrimage, I learned, was much more circuitous than the unswerving route we now travelled. His was a Christian background, but as he studied, scepticism, unbelief and secular philosophies seemed for a time to make him doubt even his own existence. For a year he was in despair, but at last met a friend who had gone through the same experience and was able to help. Stephen cried out to God, and knew God answered. Finally, he was ready to commit himself to Christ.

The journey passed quickly as I listened to Stephen's

story, and soon Victor was introducing me to Lieutenant Mishra...

As a young boy in a remote Uttar Pradesh village, Mishra had been proud to watch his father perform the priestly duties which would one day be his. As a member of the Brahmin, the highest Hindu caste, he was himself being instructed in the appropriate Hindu ceremonies, and was proud of his family's position in the religious hierarchy.

While a teenager at school in Kanpur City, Mishra came into contact with some nominal Christians - but their lives did not impress him. In 1968 however he joined the navy, and met a Christian of a very different kind. His name was A.M.K. Danam. "He never drank or smoked," Mishra recalled, "and he was always reading his Bible and praying. I thought he was going to extremes, but I had to admire him."

Danam befriended Mishra, and tried to interest him in reading the Bible. "I have no intention of being converted," thought Mishra to himself. "If two hundred and fifty years of British rule weren't enough to convert my forefathers, why should I succumb now?" But Danam persevered. Finally Mishra agreed to take a look at the Christians' Scriptures - but only with the intention of finding fault, discovering foolish or inconsistent passages, and confronting Danam with them. After all, Hinduism was the *eternal* religion!

Mishra began to read:

> You have heard that it was said, Eye for eye and tooth for tooth but I tell you, do not resist an evil person..... You have heard that it was said, Love your neighbour and hate your enemy. But I tell you: love your enemies and pray for those who persecute you.
>
> (Matt. 5:38-39, 43-44)

When Mishra reached this part he was thunder-struck. Never a man spoke like this man. He read the Gospels over and over again.

Mishra marvelled at the enlightened views of Jesus. In Hinduism a man was permitted to remarry but a woman could not. Everyone accepted that the Hindu scriptures favoured the man. But Jesus was saying something totally different, and that almost two thousand years ago! He claimed that all are equal in God's sight, and, what's more, that people, not their *karmas,* are responsible for the sins they commit.

Then Mishra discovered something else. When he got to the Book of Romans he found this passage:

> Although they claimed to be wise, they became fools and exchanged the glory of the immortal God for images made to look like mortal men and birds and animals and reptiles....They exchanged the truth of God for a lie, and worshipped and served created things rather than the Creator, who is forever praised.
>
> (Romans 1:22-23, 25)

Mishra remembered how his father would go into a house in their village and read the Hindu scriptures, perform rituals and bless the family. The people would worship his father and other Brahmin priests, as well as cows, birds and snakes. Suddenly this seemed very evil.

Mishra felt in awe of God's Word and began to read it more earnestly, becoming conscious of the fact that he himself was a sinner. But he still did not like Christians. And when some believers approached him and urged him to attend some meetings, he was very resentful. "Those Christians would go to any lengths to convert us," he thought bitterly.

But very reluctantly, Mishra found himself going to the meeting - and even rather enjoying it. The speaker, Brother N.G. John, approached him at the close.

"What do you think of Christ?" the brother asked.

"Oh, I think He's wonderful. His teachings are truly

amazing," replied Mishra with feeling.

"Why then don't you accept Him as your Saviour?" the man asked gently.

But Mishra was not ready.

On July 3, 1973 Brother John visited Mishra one night on board the ship. Many of the others were out enjoying themselves. Mishra was on duty but they were able to sit down on a wooden log on the jetty, where it was quiet.

"You know so much about Jesus. What is keeping you from accepting Him?"

"I'll read the whole Bible first, and then - "

"But it's not a question of knowledge. It's a question of making a commitment. Don't you know you're a sinner?'

"Oh yes; I fully realise this - "

"Well then, you just have to ask Him for forgiveness."

Mishra said a simple prayer in Hindi, and knew the transaction was complete. "It's not so much that I've changed my religion," he told his surprised friends in the days that followed, "but Christ has changed my life." It was true; his previous desires had just melted away.

Whenever possible Mishra returned to his village and read the Bible to his friends and any others who stopped by. One day he became aware that some Brahmin priests had come to listen, and after that he was able to go in to the village temple and preach about Christ.

On leave one day, he went to another village and walked up to the temple, where he met the local priest who was staying on the premises because some ornaments belonging to the idol had been stolen a few days earlier. The priest was a well-educated man with degrees in philosophy. "If your god cannot guard himself, how can he guard you?" Mishra asked him. When the priest had no answer, Mishra explained to him the greatness and love of Christ. Before he left, Mishra handed the priest a copy of the New Testament, which he received gladly.

"Is there any change in a Hindu's life because of his religious beliefs?" he asked the villagers one day. "You try to avoid certain sins but often you do them anyway. Here is Jesus Christ who has already paid the penalty for your sin and makes it possible for you to know God intimately."

Mishra's elder brother was very much against his Christian beliefs and even more opposed to his public preaching. The Brahmins in his area became very angry and threatened him. One night he lay awake for a long time. Finally he lit a lamp and opened his Bible. He began reading:

> Though ten thousand come against me
> the Lord will sustain me.

It was all he needed. All fear fled and he went off to sleep.

In the Navy some of his friends would mock him, and often the men would want to argue. One night he said: "If Hindus believe that all gods are the same, then why do you object if I wish to worship the one called Jesus? Is He not OK, too?" In each discussion he found that there were always a few people who would listen thoughtfully. Perhaps they would want to hear more later on.

That night, in an impromptu meeting, I heard Mishra speak on the attributes of God. "Many people in this country," he began, "are content to worship 'gods' whose qualities or capabilities are not higher than their own. Indeed some of these 'gods' do not reach the standards set by most ordinary human beings. Why then should they be worshipped as 'gods'?

"Surely a true God - One who rises far above all other beings - would be an all-powerful, all-knowing Creator. He would not be made with human hands, as some 'gods' are! A true God would have the power to control the forces of nature which He had created, and have power over sickness, as well as the authority to cast out evil spirits. Such a God would know the thoughts of everyone in the world.

"A true God would be perfect, and holy. Man is born in sin, and sins with ease. It takes effort and discipline to aspire to higher, more noble thoughts. We see imperfection in ourselves and in everyone around us. But a true God would be perfect holiness, perfect justice, perfect mercy! He would be able to heal and impart life. He himself would be immortal. And a true God would be a God of love! Is this concept impossibly high? Is it an idle dream, to seek a Being with attributes so much greater than our own?

"I sought such a God, *and I found Him!* But I discovered He was far greater than anything I could have imagined. He revealed all these attributes, and more, by sending His Son Jesus Christ to earth, to demonstrate to us His power, His holiness, His knowledge, and above all, His love.

"Hindus believe that anything can be called god," Mishra said finally. "But a 'god' without these characteristics: how could he be God?"

> You praised the gods of silver and gold, of bronze, iron, wood and stone, which cannot see or hear or understand. But you did not honour the God who holds in his hand your life and all your ways.
>
> (Dan. 5:23)

It was a much quieter ride back to the city, each of us lost in our thoughts. As we approached Bombay, Victor suggested a bite to eat before we went to our respective homes. The driver swung the car into the Hotel Centaur drive, and we climbed out and walked through the wide lobby. I glanced over my shoulder at the jewellery and gift shops, glittering reminders of earlier visits. They didn't seem so important now.

FIVE

A search for joy

Come, O Lord, and stir our hearts.
Call us back to Yourself. Kindle
Your fire in us and carry us away.
Let us scent Your fragrance and
take Your sweetness.

Saint Augustine
Confessions

The young nun looked at her superior. "I'm not coming back," she said gently.

Resl had entered the convent as soon as she left school.

"I wanted to tell people about God," she was to tell me later, "and the only way I knew how was to become a nun." And now fourteen years later, Resl was leaving for the same reason: to tell others about Jesus....

Her time at the convent had begun with two and a half years training, followed by teacher training and theological studies. The community had developed an interest in Indian philosophy with a view to Indianising forms of worship and Resl found herself studying Hindu forms of prayer, yoga and Buddhist meditation. Soon her vision and her own inner peace began to fade. The more she studied other gods and other religious forms the more she realised she was desperately seeking her own peace and fulfilment.

She went to Varanasi on a study camp. Here she discovered the *yogis* - holy men - on the banks of the Ganga, and got up at 2 am to visit the river bank, eager to find peace. But what she found was jarring noise and jostling crowds. As for the yogis, some had objects drilled through their tongues or screws put through their hands. None had anything to share with Resl. She travelled to Sarnath and Bodh Gaya where it was said Buddha had found his enlightenment. Here she observed monks sitting in the lotus positions. But no one could tell her how to find peace with God.

Resl received a B.A. in Philosophy from Bombay University in 1970. But she was becoming increasingly depressed and the deception and guilt of a furtive love affair only added to the pressures. She was given tablets to sleep and tablets to keep awake, and battled constantly with thoughts of suicide.

One day as she was on her way to a school picnic, Resl noticed a large ship called the *Logos* docked in Bombay harbour. Remembering an earlier invitation to visit the ship she decided to stop off and go on board. As she approached she saw many young people manning the bookstall and exhibitions. From the very first minute she was struck by the joy on every face. It looked so natural, so much a part of them. A beautiful Swedish girl, Irma Svennson, came up and introduced herself. At once Resl said, "Tell me one thing. What makes you all so happy? What has given you this joy?" The girl laughed: "It's just the love of Jesus Christ!" *That was the first time Resl had ever heard anyone say that.* Resl turned to go, and the girl called out: "Come again!" The whole thing had taken just five minutes.

A few days later an eager Resl returned to the Logos. She found herself telling Irma all about her vocation, her search and her depression. One question Irma kept asking then and later in letters when she left Bombay was, "When was the exact date you accepted Jesus as your Lord and Saviour?" Resl couldn't give an answer.

When Irma returned to Bombay, Resl went excitedly to the Operation Mobilisation compound to meet her. As they talked about Resl's resentment toward some of the nuns and her inability to feel forgiveness, Irma explained the simple message of Jesus Christ: whoever we are, learned or illiterate, religious or infidel, rich or poor, we need to approach God as sinners who can be cleansed only by the shed blood of Jesus. Jesus died not only to take away sin but to free us from depression and hatred. Irma explained that once we approach God in this way, our sins will be forgiven. It is like being born all over again. "To live 'in the flesh'," Irma told her, "is to tolerate bitterness, hatred and other ill feelings. But when the Holy Spirit comes into one's life, He implants the characteristics of Christ Himself: forgiveness, love and peace.

"You know, Resl, right now the Lord Jesus is waiting to give you this new life. It's not a list of religious rules; it is the person of Jesus taking your life in His. Even now He says:

> Here I am! I stand at the door and knock.
> If anyone hears my voice and opens the
> door, I will come in and eat with him, and
> he with Me."
>
> (Rev. 3:20)

And so on 16 October, 1975 in the OM compound, sitting on a broken bench under the trees, Resl, a professed nun for fourteen years, at last discovered new life in Christ. That night she slept like a baby, without tablets or any medication.

She began to read the Bible and to find answers to her remaining questions. In Romans 8 she read that there is "no condemnation for those who are in Christ Jesus... who do not live according to the sinful nature but according to the Spirit." Here too she discovered the amazing way in which "God works in all things for the good of those who love Him, who have been called according to His purpose...." Resl began to share these discoveries with the other nuns and Bible studies were started. Many of the nuns came to a new birth experience at this time, finding for themselves Jesus as their personal Saviour.

Although Resl's health was daily improving, her doctor recommended a one year leave of absence, and that she should be sent home to rest. This was remarkable because never in the history of the one hundred year old community had anyone been granted a leave of absence.

Towards the end of her leave, Resl returned to the convent to make a retreat with some other nuns in a suburb of Bombay. "Whatever it cost," she told me later, "I was eager to do what God wanted. I had really fallen in love with Him."

One day while praying, Resl began thinking: "If I left the convent, I couldn't afford to study." It was something she loved dearly. The Scriptures brought her reply:

> But whatever was to my profit I now consider loss for the sake of Christ. What is more, I consider everything a loss compared to the surpassing greatness of knowing Christ Jesus my Lord, for whose sake I have lost all things.
>
> (Phil. 3:7-8)

"If I leave the convent," she thought again, "I shall need to start work." With that thought came the verse:

> But seek first His kingdom and His righteousness, and all these things will be given to you as well. Therefore do not worry about tomorrow, for tomorrow will worry about itself.
>
> (Matt. 6:33-34)

"If I leave the convent," she prayed finally, "I'll want to speak about You, but people may think I left as a failure. Won't that be letting You down?"

In her heart she heard a voice say, "I don't need you to defend Me."

"OK, Lord," she prayed, "if You want me to leave, I'll go."

Suddenly the whole room seemed filled with the fragrance of blossoms. She looked out of the window at the barren, treeless landscape. Perhaps someone had brought some flowers into the room. She whispered to the nun at her side, "Can you smell the blossoms?"

The sister looked at her curiously: "I can't smell anything." Then Resl knew it was the presence of the Lord.

The community was shocked at her decision. It was unprecedented for a solemnly professed nun to leave the convent. Papers were sent to the Vatican and Belgium: her petition had to be cleared with Rome. Letters came back asking her to reconsider. But Resl knew what she must do.

Resl officially belonged to the convent until a day in 1977 when she said goodbye to her sisters. "The doors of the convent will always be open to you," they told her as she departed. Resl thanked them for their love: she had no regrets for those years.

Now at home, Resl had a great desire to study the Word of God, and was praying one day for guidance about her future. Some days later, she received a letter from a friend who had gone to Capernwray Bible School in England. "Why don't you come here too?" she asked. When Resl looked at the date of the letter, she saw it had been written on the very day she had been praying!

After that, the miraculous began to happen. The girl in England sent Resl her air fare. An anonymous stranger bequeathed to Capernwray a sum to support an Indian student. People began to slip gifts of money into her letter-box. Resl's Heavenly Father met every need of those years of study and travel.

And then one day, at an open air meeting in a slum back in India, she met her husband to be, Sarat.

Like Resl, Sarat was brought up in a Catholic home. Once at college in Bombay, however, Sarat began to enjoy his new-found freedom. "It was a wonderful feeling," he recalls, "to be free to do my own thing. Suddenly I felt no compulsion to believe in God. Why was I a Christian anyway, and not a Hindu or a Parsi? They were content with their faith because it was how they were brought up. I was called a Christian, I reasoned, because my parents had me baptised when I was too young to know the difference - without my consent, too!"

His doubts grew as he looked out of his window and saw the slums. "What or who decides these things?" he wondered. "I could see these people: born in poverty, living in poverty, dying in poverty. What hope did they have of ever getting out of their situation? I came to the conclusion that if God existed at all, He must be a cruel God."

In case the Christians were right, however, Sarat

continued to attend church. "At that point I defined myself as an agnostic," he said. "It was fashionable to be leftist, and to read Laski and Marx."

At this time Sarat's mother contracted cancer. *"Why?"* he asked he-knew-not-who. Why should a good person like her have the sword of Democles hanging over her head? He saw his lovely mother waste away.

He did a course in yoga, longing for peace, but it didn't help. All this while he continued to attend church, to please the family and to be acceptable in society. Around this time he graduated in Chemistry and then did post-graduate studies in marketing management at Bombay University.

One day he attended a meeting in which a new priest was speaking about life in the Spirit. He was narrating an incident in John's Gospel:

> The disciples asked Jesus, "Rabbi, where
> are you staying?" He said to them, "Come
> and see."

> (John 1:38-39)

The priest said: "Forget all you've heard about the 'charismatic renewal'. We are not going to talk about a movement, or a religion. We simply want you to *come and see* Jesus Christ for yourself. He wants to give you life in His Spirit."

Sarat was touched by the priest's sincerity and honesty. *Come and see.* It seemed an invitation to him personally.

That night he stopped for a moment before getting into bed. "If You're there, show me!" he told God.

Sarat attended the next meeting in the series. He sat in the back of the hall smoking, and enjoyed the group who sang at the beginning. Then it was 'testimony time' and various women lined up to speak.

It was absolutely crazy. Never had Sarat heard such nonsense! One woman said they had no gas cylinder in the house and then one turned up. Another told of her worries when a crowded bus approached, and how thankful she was to God when it stopped right in front of her. Sarat was totally shocked. How naive these Christians were! As if God was concerned about her getting on a crowded bus! Imagine, he fumed, crediting Jesus with that! As a scientist, he put it down to coincidence. He was confident that he - not they - had the proper perspective.

Then the priest began to talk again. He spoke of Jesus on the Cross. This was nothing new to Sarat. He'd had years and years of this at boarding school. The priest continued, speaking now of a relationship with Christ. Well that was certainly new, Sarat thought. There was daily mass at school, but here was a priest speaking about 'receiving Jesus in your heart'.

"Think about it," the priest said, telling them that Jesus was standing at the door and knocking.

"OK, I've thought about it," Sarat said to himself. "I'll pursue fame and fortune first and then think about God and religion at age sixty-five."

Then the priest said: "But if you are a young person who thinks you can offer your life to God in your old age - you're just giving him *the bones.*"

That night at home, Sarat knelt by his bed. "Jesus, if you are God," he prayed, "and you need my permission to come into my heart, go ahead."

The next day, Sarat realised that he wasn't smoking. He soon became aware of a hunger to read the Bible daily. He discovered he was healed of a long-standing psychological problem, and he began to spend hours in prayer. His family would bang on his door at mealtimes. "Are you still in there?" they'd shout. To a priest, his bewildered father complained: "He's praying all the time!"

Wanting to make a clean breast of his old life, Sarat wrote all his sins down on two foolscap pieces of paper. He took them to the renewal priest, who looked at the list, and then at Sarat, and smiled. "You haven't missed anything, have you? Let's pray and ask the Lord to forgive you." Later Sarat was baptised in the Holy Spirit, just as the disciples had been at Pentecost.

When Resl and Sarat were married, they wanted their wedding to be truly Christian. After the exchange of vows, the congregation prayed over them, and Sarat spoke at the reception of how both Resl's searching and his struggling led to the same person, Jesus Christ. A gospel booklet was distributed to each guest as a thankyou from the bridal couple.

Now Sarat works as a sales manager for a petroleum company in Bombay and has learnt the Biblical principle of tithing. Grateful for all God had given him - forgiveness, new life, love - he began to give of his substance. In time he was amazed to see that his salary had increased *four times* since he began to tithe!

"The Lord has guided us every day of our marriage," Sarat said, looking at Resl with a smile. "Life has not always been easy, but we really feel the tangible presence of the Lord."

We finished talking and were deeply conscious of that Presence.

SIX

The true flavour of being Indian

Lead me from the unreal to the real.
Lead me from darkness to light.
Lead me from death to immortality....

Brihad Aranyaka
Upanishad

Chandu Wakankar is Education Officer for the World Wild Life Fund India, and based in Bombay. He is an intelligent man with a wide range of interests including mountaineering and reading, especially Indian history. He also has a love of classical Indian music, and speaks with an infectious enthusiasm for his subject - whether it be Indian history, wild life or philosophy.

Chandu's mother's ancestors were nobles in the courts of the *Peshwas*, the ruling class who resisted the coming of the British. In more recent times his grandfather took part in the resistance movement against the British, suffering imprisonment for his activities. With this heritage Chandu readily embraced the idealism of the post-independence period when he was growing up in a Brahmin Hindu family in Bombay. He has, like others in his generation, strong feelings of patriotism, pride in his country and optimism about its future. The early days of independence aroused a growing sense of social and cultural identity. This new sense of belonging developed a desire for social reform and a practical idealism. Young people like Chandu recognised the need to absorb as much learning as possible and then to use it to the benefit of the country. Seeing that each new period offers opportunities for improvement and advancement, they were eager to take up the challenge.

Chandu's own quest for learning was encouraged particularly by the personal attention and interesting manner of one of his High School teachers. He was a simple country man whose accent was not as sophisticated as that of the cultured youths he taught, who often imitated his voice and joked about him. This man was a Christian.

"Christ was absolutely unique," the teacher said one day, "the only sinless person."

"How can you say that?" the boys argued, "when there are so many great philosopher-saints?"

Chandu agreed with the others but he enjoyed listening to the Bible stories. Jesus' life was one of such humility, courage and sacrifice that he concluded Christ must surely be one of the great saints.

As the years passed, Chandu the teenager began to think for himself and was puzzled about the lives of his Hindu gods. How could they act as they did and still be gods? Some were polygamous; others approved of caste. At various times some committed deeds unworthy of godhood. Chandu realised that the enlightened Indians of the day aspired to higher standards than this. Surely gods should set an example to mankind?

Nevertheless Chandu did not consider Jesus Christ as an alternative to the Hindu gods. When watching street preaching by Indian Christians, the young Chandu thought with contempt that they were commercialising religion: that they were selling it like soap or any other commodity.

When Chandu entered college he began to read science in earnest. He became fascinated with the subject as he read of discoveries in astronomy and physics. One book said that the universe was billions of years old: this surely disproved all the religious myths. He could see no path better than that of atheism. Surely religion was an outdated thing, he concluded, in the face of modern science.

"I stopped going to worship at that time," Chandu remembers. "If I ever went to the temple, it would be to please my family. I'd just toss a flower, for the sake of form."

Chandu was attracted to a girl with a Brahmin name but she turned out to be from a converted Christian family. Chandu had too much self-respect to pursue that friendship. "I would not stoop so low," he told friends, "as to change my religion just to marry a girl!"

In Chandu's second year of college he met up with Viju Abraham and other Christian believers who had meetings together. His first encounter with this group hadn't been so fruitful. One of their number, Danny, caught Chandu on the terrace of their hostel one evening and spoke earnestly to him about God, Christ and sin.

"I was impatient with him," Chandu told me. "I told him bluntly that I was an atheist and didn't accept what he said. I argued that if God existed then sin would also exist. If sin existed, then the thought of sin would be just as bad. It would be a hopeless situation!"

Chandu concluded that what Christians called 'sin' was simply any anti-social act that disrupted the social fabric and therefore was something to be avoided. He thought it was more profitable to seek to improve the quality of life in society, and not to evoke guilt in individuals for 'sinful' thoughts or acts.

But Chandu and Viju got to know each other better during his third year of college. He accepted invitations to attend gospel meetings, enjoying the snacks, the friendliness and the warm welcome. Of course there was the inevitable sermon, with visiting speakers reading from the Bible and setting out their views. Chandu didn't care much for these.

After one such gospel meeting Chandu couldn't resist arguing back and forth with the speaker. He finally told the man: "If God exists and shows Himself to me in any manner, I will believe Him."

The speaker replied: " If you are honest about this, He will honour it."

Chandu took up this challenge, and found himself praying aloud: "God, if you exist, please reveal Yourself to me. You may do so by sight or sound, or just to my heart. But please reveal Yourself in some way to me."

Chandu thought about this on the train returning from the meeting. He had meant this prayer even though his feelings remained the same. He took from his pocket a booklet he had been given earlier in the evening entitled *Starting from Zero in the Quest for God.* He opened it to the first page, and read these words:

> If modern man were asked to believe the
> following statement, he would accept it... "If

> any man would come to *science*, he must
> believe that *science* is, and that *it* is the
> rewarder of them that diligently seek *it*..."

Chandu looked closely at that statement and thought hard. As a scientist, he assumed the universe operated by consistent laws. He believed the human mind capable of understanding these laws, so that when two or more sane minds interpreted phenomena rightly, their explanations would coincide and a rare discovery would be made.

"If I must first believe these fundamental notions of science," he reasoned, "before I can understand and benefit from it, then *I must also first believe in God in the same way!*"

Right then and there Chandu made an act of will: that he would believe in God. And strangely, at once he knew in his heart that God was *there*.

That night he returned to the hostel believing in God, championing Him instead of the atheism he had professed an hour earlier. He mentioned this openly to his atheist friends, who were amazed at his reversal. "What made you change?" they asked.

Chandu eagerly presented to them the ideas that had come into his mind on the train. He was surprised they did not find his logic helpful!

"You must first *will* to believe," he insisted. "An African tribesman, seeing a telephone for the first time, may laugh at the instrument. But if he's willing to accept the possibility that it works and try it out, he'll discover the truth of it."

If only they were willing to open the door slightly, the ensuing ray of light would encourage them to let more light in, Chandu reasoned, though not yet a Christian. He returned to the Hindu scriptures, and a day or two later found himself in a lively discussion with Christians who insisted that the idea of a transcendent God was a Biblical one. Chandu paraphrased the Gita which said that idols were worshipped by natural people, but that "enlightened souls seek God in an all pervading eternal self." Their arguments could not convince Chandu that Christianity was the only path to truth.

One night, however, his friends went off to a meeting;

although they didn't ask him to join them he almost forced himself on them. It turned out to be a prayer meeting, and at one point Chandu too prayed aloud. "God, You have revealed yourself to me, but I don't know how to come to You. I think all ways lead to You. If You show me that this is so, I'll accept that. But if You show me that there's only one way, I'll come that way. I do want to give the rudder of my life to You."

A few weeks later when the academic year had ended and the other students had left to return home, Chandu was wandering through the empty hostel rooms and idly picked up a magazine. In it was an article about the flesh trade. It quoted a verse from the *Skandha Puran* that mentioned the battles between gods and demons during which many gods died, leaving their widows without livelihood. Thus the rishis and sages advised the widows to undertake the flesh trade.

"I had my questions about the Hindu gods," Chandu told me, "going back to my school days. This verse seemed to confirm my suspicions that the gods of Hinduism, even if charismatic figures, were only human beings. I was in a vacuum, aware that Hinduism had not shown me the true God.

Although restless at the time with disappointments in his scholastic work, Chandu was not depressed. "I was certainly not rushing out to seek solace in another religion," he said. "I was still a rational being."

He began to ask himself, "If there is no true god in Hinduism, where can it be?" He thought the Bible might help, but he didn't know where to look, and his Christian friends had all gone home. And so he prayed: "God, I'll open this book but You will have to direct me to the right place."

He looked down at the Bible, and it opened to Matthew chapter 5, *The Sermon on the Mount.* The title evoked memories of the passage he'd learned the year before in his English class. But it also brought back to his mind the film *Ben Hur.* He had been quite struck by the personality of Christ in that film. The viewer never saw His face, but the presence and influence of Jesus were keenly felt.

Chandu read:

> You have heard that it was said to the
> people long ago: do not murder, and
> anyone who murders will be subject to
> judgment. But I tell you that anyone who is
> angry with his brother will be subject to
> judgment....
> You have heard that it was said, do not
> commit adultery. But I tell you that anyone
> who looks at a woman lustfully has already
> committed adultery with her in his heart....
>
> (Matt. 5:21-22, 27-28)

"This is what my conscience has been telling me all these years!" marvelled Chandu when he read that. Nowhere in any other philosophy had he seen this preached! In no other man had he seen it lived!

"Only Jesus has done this," he murmured. "*So He is God..and no one else...*" With tears in his eyes, he knelt down. He knew nothing about redemption, or resurrection, or judgment. He knew only that he was away from God, and that *Christ was God.* He said, "Make me your child...."

And God did.

The next day Chandu went home and told his father. To his joy his father did not object to his becoming a Christian, and even gave his permission for Chandu to be baptised. But afterwards the news spread and many Hindu friends and associates were disturbed. There were some rumours that he wanted to marry a Christian or that he wanted a scholarship to study in America.

Chandu's father observed his friends' reaction and said to him: "You can remain a Christian if you want to, but just call yourself a Hindu."

Chandu said he couldn't do this; it would be tantamount to lying to God as well as to man. His father asked Chandu whether he planned to change his name. "No," Chandu replied, "God does not ask us to change our outward forms, or to give up our nation or culture or family." He told his father that he was proud of these things and would not want to alter them. His father said: "Could you just call yourself a Hindu on official forms?"

It seemed a last attempt at compromise, but Chandu felt this was impossible. In exasperation his father said that in that case he must leave home! Chandu went, reluctantly and regretfully, saying he'd come back whenever they wanted.

He returned to the hostel, a homeless person. His friend Viju tried to find him a room. The warden, a nominal Christian who had had no such spiritual experience of his own, felt very embarrassed and uncomfortable with Chandu whenever he spoke of his new faith.

At home, Chandu's mother broke down. His father sought the advice of a close friend who said, "Don't throw your son out because of this. Hasn't he expressed his love and respect for you? Better to inquire *why* he became a Christian." And so his father relented and invited Chandu to return home, which he did.

"Since then," Chandu told me, "without in any way compromising my faith, I have been able to identify myself absolutely with my family, my culture and my country. I guess I'm not a copy-book Christian," he grinned at me over coffee. "I've had a great love for the physical sciences, for climbing and for reading. Often hobbies like mountaineering have kept me away from church attendance. I continue to read Indian history and to develop my love of classical Indian music. I'm still finding out more about the terrain of my country, and more and more I enjoy the true flavour of being Indian...."

SEVEN

Out of the fox's jaws

They cried to You and were saved,
they trusted and were not
disappointed.

Psalm 22:5

I was back in Bangalore, and I recalled my first visit when we had stayed at a beautiful guest house overhung with bougainvillaea. On that occasion I had been taken on a tour of the centre, with its municipal buildings magnificently carved in pink marble.

Bangalore is also known for its Christian heritage. It has two hundred and fifty churches, representing fifteen denominations, and over seven per cent of its inhabitants claim to be Christians. Among the six hundred or more Christian organisations, schools and missions in the city are hospitals, bookshops and printing establishments.

One of these missions is EFICOR, the Evangelical Fellowship of India's Committee on Relief. In disaster or depressed areas, in slums or in villages, EFICOR workers share the love of Christ in a tangible way.

One such is Krickwin Marak. He and his lovely wife Hmingi come from the North East of India, Krickwin from a Garo tribe and Hmingi from a Mizo tribe in Mizoram. She greeted me at the door wearing a beautiful wrap-around skirt woven in a Naga red tartan and with her baby daughter fastened to her back in a sling, which is the way of the hill people.

"I was born somewhere around 1950," Krickwin began. "We didn't use a calendar in those days in our tribe. Our people were simple farmers, animists from Meghalaya, although my ancestors came from Tibet."

He was from the hill country described by Rudyard Kipling as the 'home of elephants'. When he was just three weeks old, his father was killed by a tiger and Krickwin was left under the care of his mother and two older brothers, who had become Christians years earlier after going to a nearby Sunday School.

One day when he was about four years old, his twenty year old brother took him to the fields as a companion. Quite suddenly storms came, hailstones fell and Krickwin's brother swept him up and rushed to the nearest big tree for shelter. There was no point in trying to run home; it was two or three kilometres away. The child watched in fear and wonder as his brother began to pray in the name of Jesus, at the same time covering the small body with his own. Suddenly the hailstorm stopped. Even the rains ceased. The two brothers ran home in safety.

But as soon as they arrived at the little house, the hailstorm returned! It was Krickwin's first recollection of a God who answers prayer.

After that he loved to hear the stories his brothers told him about Jesus, who loved people and healed the sick. Many a night the three of them would sit in a darkened corner of the house, telling and retelling the old stories to each other.

Their father had been very much opposed to his sons' interest in Christianity. After his death, their mother felt there wasn't much she could do about *their* beliefs, but she felt Krickwin was still young enough to control. And she didn't intend to allow *him* to run after that strange foreign teaching.

On January 11, 1963, a wild fox attacked several people in the neighbouring village. Some road construction workmen from Bihar were killed, and a neighbour was attacked and later died. Krickwin was walking in the field that day when he saw the fox coming for him. The twelve year old boy fell down as he tried to escape. He cried and kicked with all his might at the savage fox, but it grasped his toes with his teeth and chewed at his ankles.

"God, please help me!" Krickwin cried out. He had been taught to pray by his brothers many years earlier, and now it came to him instinctively.

The fox suddenly stopped his attack. Miraculously

Krickwin, although badly injured, was able to scramble up a nearby tree. The fox looked up at the terrified boy, then turned and went away! Krickwin remained in the tree, bleeding badly from his mangled feet, shivering and in shock. But he kept praying. Finally he climbed slowly down the tree and crawled all the way home.

There were no medical facilities in such an isolated area. Krickwin's mother could only watch and worry that first week. Others came to look and whisper. They knew what had happened to the others.

For ten days he lay on the bed, weak and in pain from his ravaged toes and ankles. But it gave him plenty of time to think. "All I want to do in my life," he finally said to his mother, "is to become a Christian."

She looked at her youngest son and softened. "If your life is spared," she told him, "yes, you can; and I will, too!"

Krickwin was walking with the help of a stick by the end of the month. The following month he attended a Christian gathering nearby and was baptised after publicly declaring his trust in Jesus Christ. That same year Krickwin's mother and sister and brother-in-law, some aunts and uncles, also decided to leave the old ways and follow Jesus.

"Six years later, during my final year at school, I had a wonderful experience," Krickwin told me that afternoon.

He had gone to a Fellowship Group meeting some distance from his village. "One evening we heard a testimony about a man who had a paralysing disease, and was healed by the power of God. We were all challenged to commit our lives more fully to Jesus Christ that night. I went to my bed but I couldn't sleep. I kept praying and crying. It seemed that my heart was bursting with new love and understanding for the Lord Jesus." Krickwin couldn't wait to get home, and rushed back eighty-six kilometres to tell his mother. From then on, greater understanding grew in his heart of the continual presence of Jesus with him.

Krickwin's new spiritual power not only blessed himself but created a response in the entire family, as had his conversion six years earlier. He was again leading the way, sharing with them a new power that the Holy Spirit could give them.

Krickwin had realised that his widowed mother could not be expected to support him after he finished high school. He therefore took a government office job in Shillong and began to study at nights toward a science degree, with a view to a career in engineering. But his heart was not at peace! Particularly after hearing a testimony one evening from an Australian lady missionary staying in Shillong, he knew what God wanted him to do. He wanted him to enter the Christian ministry.

Krickwin knew only too well what this would mean. No regular income.... no material security....regarded by the world as no more than an impoverished itinerant preacher. "Many could not understand," he admitted, "why I would throw away my opportunities in this way. Some felt it was my duty to support my mother. Others believed I should try to make a career for myself. Some Christians did not agree with my decision to study for Christian service." But others did and one group committed themselves to supporting him through his four years of study.

In November 1977 a cyclone blew into Andhra Pradesh, killing thirty thousand people and destroying cattle and houses. Krickwin read about EFICOR and their project to aid the stricken villages. EFICOR workers dug for drinking water, helped to rebuild houses and gave practical assistance where it was most needed. Several years later he felt God's leading to join EFICOR and before long found himself doing similar work - surveying needs, giving practical assistance - in other areas where disaster struck.

"Shortly after joining EFICOR," Krickwin recalled, "I was sent to a village in Andhra Pradesh to supervise a building project. The people seemed very suspicious and even hostile. I was new and nervous, and I couldn't speak Telagu. I thought, "How can I communicate with these people? I had a job to do: practical work that would demonstrate our love without words. But I could not withhold the clear message of Christ which would bring Light to those who wanted it."

Several days after he arrived in the village he felt he had

to try to convey this to the villagers. That evening he lit his petrol lamp at the door of his tent and spoke through the interpreter: "I'm a Christian and this is the way I worship my God. Each evening at this time I'll put everything else aside and speak to Him - and listen to Him, too. Please don't be offended at what I do. In fact, if you wish to come and join me, you may do so."

Each evening from then on, people began to congregate outside Krickwin's tent. He found he was able to talk about the love of God to them. Each evening they listened carefully. And the next evening, they'd return.

One night some women came to the tent, chattering excitedly. He stopped talking for a moment and asked what the trouble was. Someone said: "They want to bring a neighbour who's demon possessed, so you can pray to your God for her."

The women reappeared, pulling a fearsome looking creature and motioning to Krickwin to take charge. The moment they handed her over to him, they fled back into their houses and slammed the doors tight! They wanted to be sure that when the demon came out, it didn't enter *their* houses!

Krickwin realised that all eyes were upon him. He knew that he could not refuse to pray for the woman. But he had never done such a thing before. What if it didn't work? What would they say? They'd think his God couldn't - or wouldn't - answer his prayer! They'd never believe in Jesus Christ then.... The answer stirred within him: *You are not alone here.*

His hand was still trembling when he placed it on the woman's head and began to pray. He thought of all the incidents in the Bible when Jesus prayed with demoniacs. Didn't they always cry with a loud voice when the demons were expelled? Didn't they fall on the ground? Krickwin kept praying over the weeping woman. Nothing seemed to happen and, as he prayed audibly for the woman and her needs, he prayed silently and earnestly for more faith to believe for a miracle.

He prayed for five or ten minutes then stopped, inwardly disappointed that there was no change. The woman turned away and the crowd kept milling about, watching and murmuring. He didn't do any more talking that night.

The next morning before dawn, he awoke to a commotion outside his tent. One of his helpers burst in on him. "The lady you prayed for last night," he said excitedly, "she's healed!"

And it was true. He met with the woman - now calm and clear-headed - and her husband later that afternoon, and he was able to share with them the Good News of Jesus, who not only heals but saves. "After that, the villagers became very friendly," said Krickwin. "There was a good co-operative spirit within the community and we were able to do all the building and repair work within two months. When we were ready to leave," he laughed, "they tried to hide our luggage so we'd have to stay!"

Krickwin and Hmingi met at Bible college. They were both preparing for Christian service and seeking God's will for their lives.

"Krickwin and I became good friends," Hmingi told me shyly. "Then one day he wrote asking me to consider whether God might want us to be together."

I asked Hmingi about her own background, and she told me that her people originally came from Burma. Her grandparents followed the tribal traditions and sacrificed to the spirits. But in the 1950's, some Christians came to her village and told the people of the God who loved the world so much that He gave His Son. This revelation came very forcibly to some, who then appealed to others. And since there was a very strong communal feeling in the tribe, they all agreed to commit themselves to Christ.

The tribe have suffered many hardships in recent years, with political unrest causing restrictions and curfews, and they have often had to move from place to place. But despite those hardships, Hmingi grew up in a happier and more peaceable world than her parents did. From her earliest years she knew she was part of a Christian family, and did not need to fear the spirit world as her ancestors had done. She attended all the church meetings, faithfully memorised scripture and always managed to win a prize at the Bible memory competitions.

As she entered her teens, however, she began to experience certain worries and anxieties. Sometimes at night she would hear the rumble of storms approaching and hear the clatter of the first hailstones on the fragile bamboo-and-thatch dwelling. She lay there terrified that the storm would come and destroy all that she held dear. Often this fear would be overlaid with bits of Bible lessons. "Maybe it's the Second Coming of Christ," she'd wonder, frightened at the possibility that she'd be left behind.

On September 8, 1969 Hmingi was invited to a youth campaign. What she heard there was not really so different from the talks and sermons she had heard throughout her young life. But there was one difference. That night the Holy Spirit gently prodded her to think where she stood personally in relation to Jesus Christ. And she found herself asking the question: *Am I outside of Christ?*

The following morning, just before setting off for school, Hmingi sat in her room and opened her Bible. She began to read,

> As evening fell, Jesus said to His disciples,
> "Let's cross to the other side of the lake."
> So they took Him just as He was and
> started out, leaving the crowds behind....
>
> (Mark 4:35-36)

Her eyes seemed glued to that spot! She began seeing something new about that passage that she had not thought of before. *Christ took them to another shore*: away from the confusion of the crowds. Her mind and spirit often felt confused by the pressures of the world. *But now He takes me just as I am*, she thought in surprise, and suddenly all her fears and burdens disappeared! From that day on, life took on a new meaning. Jesus was there with her, helping, guiding and giving her peace.

In her area lived an old man named Chawngkhunga, well-known for wandering around in rags most of the time.

Sometimes people would give him better clothing, and then see him still dressed in the same old rags. "What did he do with that clothing?" they'd wonder, annoyed. But old Chawngkhunga never wanted anything for himself. He would give away any gift he received. He may have been despised and misunderstood, but underneath those rags was a heart that loved the Saviour. And surprisingly, he wrote beautiful poetry and hymns that would live on long after he was gone.

Hmingi remembered one of those hymns. These days she sang it to herself as she was discovering more and more the truth of those beautiful words.

>Oh gracious God
>the joy You have given to me
>within my heart
>is beyond the understanding
>of the wisdom of the world.
>
>The wisdom of a wise man
>cannot comprehend
>Oh Saviour
>the depth of Your mystery.
>How deep and high
>is the love of God:
>Higher than the wisdom of the
>world
>it fills heaven and earth.
>
>To me,
>a lost sinner
>He gives me life
>through the Spirit.
>Bless the Lord
>oh my soul.

"From then on," said Hmingi, her lovely eyes shining, "I became very burdened for my family." Although part of a Christian community, many of them lacked a personal experience of Jesus Christ. Hmingi began to pray for them in earnest. At first it was difficult to talk about her faith, but gradually her confidence grew.

As she finished high school she sensed more and more that she would be involved in Christian work. Already her church was using her to teach the children and young people. After Hmingi completed her college course in Lunglei, she went to Yavatmal for Bible training to study for the B.D. degree. Her church agreed to support her financially, and on completion of her studies she would return there and work for them.

Then Krickwin Marak came back into the picture.

"How did you know that God was directing you together?" I asked her. "Did everything fall neatly into place for you?"

"Oh no," she smiled, "it wasn't as easy as that. There were many complications. We had to do a lot of praying, and trusting. We believed God wanted us to marry, but at first my mother wasn't so sure. Then we had to accept my responsibilities to my home church who had supported me. Krickwin was in Assam; I would be in Mizoram, by road a journey taking four days."

"How did you overcome these obstacles?" I asked.

"When you want God's direction, you can't attempt to work things out for yourself. That's using the 'wisdom of the world'. You must first of all acknowledge that *God is sovereign*: we exist because of Him! We should seek to discover the mind of the Lord. We must then trust in His wisdom and His timing. This sometimes requires patience. For the first two years of our marriage I continued to work in Mizoram, while Krickwin was in Assam. We were only able to visit each other at three monthly intervals."

"That must have been terrible!" I exclaimed.

"The Lord was in control," Hmingi said firmly. "It is the cost of discipleship, and, after all, He has done so much for us!"

"There's another poem, also composed by Chawngkhunga," she said, "which is one of my favourites..."

Even if I am
surrounded by fire and flood,
I will still go on.
The glory of the world
will obstruct my way no more,
for I have my salvation in Christ.

I will be afraid of Judgment no more,
for the Father has accepted me.

EIGHT

More than the Asian Games

*Jesus said, 'Simon son of John, do
you truly love me more than these?'
'Yes Lord,' he said, 'You know that I
love You.' Jesus said, 'Feed my lambs....'*

John 21:15

I first heard of Robin Paul, his sporting achievements and
his Christian faith, through *Christians in Sport*. This
organisation, a UK-based fellowship of Christian athletes,
helped to arrange a cricket tour of India by members of the
group. Robin was involved in the preparations and the tour
took place recently, a great success.

Robin was born in Bangalore of a Bengali Hindu father
and a Christian mother. His parents separated when Robin
was very young and after that he, his mother and sister
started to attend the Methodist Church. When Robin was
seventeen, he began to run. He was at Baldwin Boys' High
School by this time and achieved a record one hundred
metre run there in 1966 which remains unbroken. He
began his sports career in earnest during his college days,
representing the state in the National Games and also his
college. During this time he won the one hundred and two
hundred metres at the All India Inter-University meets in
1969/70.

Success on the track brought satisfaction and also a
certain amount of fame and popularity. But Robin began to
wonder whether he had overlooked something of
significance in life.

At school as a lad of eight, Robin had attended a
Scripture Union camp and responded when the speaker
invited boys to 'give their lives to Jesus Christ.' No doubt he
meant this, but it hadn't revolutionised his thinking at that
early stage.

In February 1970 during his last year at university, he

attended a missionary meeting at which Ian North was the speaker. Feeling challenged and disturbed, he rushed off to a university dance and tried to push all thoughts of the talk from his mind. But the music and gaiety didn't manage to blot out the deep stirrings that were going on in his heart. At 2 a.m. he sat down on a step and 'surrendered'. He committed his life - and his running - to Christ.

The Bible teacher, Dr. Ken Gnanakan, became a good friend and adviser. He encouraged him to read the Bible every day. Robin learned at this time that just as a runner needs to train and exercise daily to develop properly, a Christian can only mature by regular sessions with the Word of God:

> Therefore since we are surrounded by such a great cloud of witnesses, let us throw off everything that hinders and the sin that so easily entangles, and let us run with perseverance the race marked out for us. Let us fix our eyes on Jesus, the author and perfector of our faith.
>
> (Heb. 12:1-2)

After obtaining his B.Sc. and during graduate study, Robin was offered a job with the firm of Tata in Jamshidpur. This work, in the Welfare Department, included leave for training. He accepted the post and moved there, and might have been content but for a growing conviction that he should give himself completely to the Christian ministry.

He involved himself with the youth work at the local church but this only made him more convinced that he should do this full time. His mother, now widowed, was unhappy about Robin's decision. "You don't know what it is to be a Christian and be fully in the work," she warned him. "Please wait five years!" That was difficult advice for Robin to accept. He recalled Jesus' words:

> Anyone who loves his father or mother more than Me is not worthy of Me!
>
> (Matt. 10:37)

It seemed that his duty to God came even before his duty to a parent. And if God had impressed upon him the life's work he was to follow, shouldn't he obey Him at once?

Robin's thoughts remained along these lines for a few days. And then during his Bible reading one morning he came upon Paul's letter to Timothy:

> Give proper recognition to those widows who are really in need. But if a widow has children or grandchildren, these should learn first of all to put their religion into practice by caring for their own family and so repaying their parents and grandparents, for this is pleasing to God....If anyone does not provide for his relatives, and especially for his immediate family, he has denied the faith and is worse than an unbeliever...
>
> (1 Tim. 5:3,4,8)

As soon as he read this he knew this was God's word to *him*. Both texts were true, but had different emphases. Robin knew God came first, but here God was issuing him with his own personal instructions: "Look after your mother now." Robin felt a load tumble off his back and he was at peace. He'd keep working - and running - until the orders changed.

In 1974 Robin Paul represented India in the India/Sri Lanka meet and was awarded the Bronze medal for the two hundred metres. At this time he was considered one of the four fastest runners in India. Next stop: the Asian Games in Teheran! It was the goal of any athlete at that time. Robin was to be part of a relay and the team worked to run under the qualifying time for their 'ticket to Teheran'. Despite gruelling training they found themselves a fraction outside the target time.

Then a 'short-cut' was privately proposed to the runners, an overlap in the relay runs that would shave off a valuable fraction of a second and put them into the Asian Games.

But it was Robin who was asked to break the rules! He was well aware of the pressures from other team members who'd practised for years for this opportunity. And there were pressures in his own heart. This could be his last chance for such an honour. He couldn't predict his performance four years hence.

The day came. As he read his morning portion, the question turned over and over in his mind: *"What are you going to do? What are you going to do?"* It was Psalm 17:

> As for the deeds of men - by the word of
> your lips I have kept myself from the ways
> of the violent. My steps have held to your
> paths; my feet have not slipped.
>
> (Verses 4 and 5)

"You are more to me," he finally said aloud, "than the Asian Games."

The team ran - Robin playing strictly by the book - and their result was just a fraction over the qualifying time of 40.3 seconds. They lost their ticket to Teheran.

Exactly five years after Robin's mother had urged him to wait to enter the Christian ministry, God spoke to him again. He went back to his mother and said: "I believe I'm to leave my job and train for God's work."

OK," she said at once, "now go with my blessing." Thus he left Tata and entered Bible School at Yavatmal in Maharastra.

When Robin committed his life to Jesus Christ in 1970, one of his first prayer requests was for a future life partner. Not long afterwards, three sisters were singing together in a church service. He looked at the middle one, Linda, and God seemed to say: "That's her."

"The problem was that I told her," he said, laughing. "I got the rebuff of my life!"

Robin remained convinced in the years to come and Linda remained firmly sceptical. It was another four years until Robin was able to persuade her to go out with him, but her continued indecision caused him much agony. "I had another five years of this," he told me ruefully. "Finally in 1979 I said to the Lord: 'I give up.' I couldn't go on any longer like that! I felt that day I just handed Linda over to the Lord."

Robin wrote her a letter to this effect. She had now moved to Delhi to work and he added that there was only one way now that would get them together. She could resign from her job and come home. But he was completely bowled over when she did just that! Robin and Linda were married - at last - in 1980.

That same year Robin was invited to the World Methodist Conference in England. It was an honour to be asked, but the cost was prohibitive. Nevertheless funds came in from unexpected sources and he found himself flying to Britain.

During that visit he was asked to speak at a Youth Conference held in Truro, Cornwall. The scene was an old tin mine, a spot where John Wesley spoke to large crowds two hundred years earlier. There were a thousand young people there, and Robin wondered nervously what he could possibly share of his experiences that would help them. Then he felt God reminding him: *You are more to me than the Asian Games*. He stood up there, surrounded by those youthful faces, and spoke of his highest sporting ambition, the temptation to deceive, and his final decision.

"In the years since that crisis," he confessed to me, "it had often pained me, thinking of what I'd missed. I'd done the right thing, yes; but it was still a bitter disappointment.

"Now as I shared with them these deep feelings, suddenly I was wholly liberated and delivered from my regrets. I knew now that God had used that disappointment to bring new vision and faith to those young people - and to me as well. The response in that tin mine was overwhelming. God spoke to many people that day! I went home thankful that it had all happened."

Now Robin Paul combines his pastoral role with work amongst the poor. He has spent some time overseeing a development project in villages sponsored by the Methodist Church.

"In so many villages," Robin said, "the poor are continually dependent upon one rich landowner. They get their wage which is totally inadequate; they spend it and then must borrow from the same landowner, often at high interest rates. They're never released from this cycle."

Robin's tasks included the setting up of *sanghas* or grain 'saving banks'. He has taught the villagers to form co-operatives and helped show the women more efficient ways of making provision for their families.

But his days as an active sportsman are by no means over. In his late thirties now, he looks as trim and fit as a twenty year old. Local Christian youth clubs get the benefit of his coaching and support. And in his spare time he's writing a book about Christian involvement in trade unions!

NINE

The narrow gate

*People blame me and call me
heedless; I doubt not they are
right in their blame*

Rabindrath Tagore
Gitanjali

Ambika sat by the side of the hospital bed holding her mother's hand. As they waited for the results of the tests her mother told her of a strange dream she'd had a few nights earlier.

"I dreamt that we were travelling in some beautiful mountains together, singing and going happily hand in hand. But there was a narrow crack in the mountain and suddenly you slipped into it and I couldn't see you!"

"Mother," said Ambika gently, continuing to hold her hand, "the way to life is a narrow one. I've accepted it, but you're still on the broad path." She paused and decided not to speak of her coming baptism. That might trigger off another heart attack.

"Yes, it *is* a narrow way," thought Ambika, "and hard too at times." She remembered how she had found the way...

She was born in Karnatake, a Brahmin Hindu, and her father died when she was a baby. After college she found a job in an industrial concern run by a Christian couple called Mr. and Mrs John Jacob, who were kind and helpful to all their employees whatever their rank and education. Their sincerity and love helped to soften Ambika's irritation with nominal Christians she had met whom she equated with gambling and drinking. Their parental concern meant much to her too, since she had never known her own father's love.

As well as beginning each day in the factory with Christian songs and prayers the owners held a Sunday evening meeting to which employees were invited. On one occasion Ambika became very angry with the speaker, Mr. Sathya Prakash, as he spoke against Hinduism and Rama and Krishna, saying how foolish it was to worship idols. When she argued with him, Mr. Prakash urged her to think about God while she was still young. "Furthermore," he went on, "you are overlooking sin."

"Sin?" Ambika looked up in surprise. "I'm not a sinner! I have always tried my best. I would be honest enough to confess to you if I did not."

Mr. Prakash gave Ambika a New Testament to read, and jotted down on a card the references of certain portions she should study. "See if you have come to that level," he told her kindly. "See if you are reaching that standard." Ambika accepted the New Testament and agreed to read the portions, but only for the sake of argument: she was going to have something to say to Mr Prakash. She began to read the Sermon on the Mount. It gave her an uneasy feeling. Perhaps she shouldn't have spoken like that to Mr. Prakash! The bad in her seemed to rise when she was confronted by him.

One day she began to think much about God and asked him, "Why did You take my father? I so long for fatherly love." At that point Ambika was certain she heard someone saying:

> You think you have no father. If you accept
> Me, I shall be your father.

The voice was so clear that Ambika thought it must be Mr. Jacob, walking through the hostel. But he was nowhere to be seen. "Could there really be a God?" she wondered, her heart pounding.

She was half afraid - yet the voice was so lovely. As the days wore on she thought it must be God's voice, because she heard it again:

> I will be with you always, and be a father to
> you if you will let me.

But she was still confused. One day she sat down and said to herself: "Jesus...Rama....Krishna...maybe these are different names for one God. Perhaps I should believe in God without thinking of His name. Yes," she decided, "I shall believe in God as my father!" And she had peace in her heart from then on.

Mr. Prakash was still chipping away at Ambika's resistance. "Do you accept Jesus now?" he asked her.

"No!" she said.

Then Mr. Jacob spoke one evening about sin. "You can't approach God alone," he explained. "There is always the problem of our sinful nature. That is why you must come through Christ, who took our sins upon Himself." Ambika left the session quietly and thought about those words for days.

One night she dreamt of a terrible fire. As she stood there fire was burning all around her, and then it was burning her. Although her body was burning, she was not destroyed. A hand touched her head. Ambika had this dream several times and awoke, terrified, unable to understand it. The final time she was so shattered that she couldn't speak. Finally she related the dream to a very patient and concerned Mr. and Mrs. Jacob.

Mr. Jacob said: "You are going to become a child of God; the fire indicates a cleansing. Whether you believe it or not," he looked at Ambika lovingly, "you will be a follower of Jesus Christ."

But Ambika became angry at this and stalked off. She had come so close - and then her rebellious nature rose up and turned her right round. It was a full year before she went to another meeting, this time arranged by Dr. Isaac John of the Asian Christian Academy. The speaker, Dr. Atwood, was explaining the need for repentance. Again Ambika objected to what was said. Mr. Jacob talked to her for a while but her mind was made up.

Strangely enough, after that incident her feelings about Christianity changed. She was now willing to accept that the Christians she had met through the Jacobs - Mr. Prakash and Dr. John - were very good people. And that caused her to conclude that Christianity, after all, was good.

The next Sunday Ambika attended a Communion service. The quiet worship soothed and attracted her. Then they handed bits of bread around. She thought to herself, "What's in that bread? People take it and then bow their heads, as if it had some special effect on them. It's a good thing I didn't take any!"

When the service was over she spoke about this to some Christian friends. They smiled and then explained to her the significance of the bread and wine.

"From then on my contact with Christians increased," said Ambika. "I began to conclude that they had much more happiness in their hearts than I had. I started to compare my life with theirs. They had accepted Jesus Christ as Saviour. Perhaps my fault lay in refusing Christ?"

She decided to visit a Christian community where people lived and worked together and practised their religion in their daily lives. It was arranged for her to go to Southern Asia Bible College as a guest for three days. It was here in that same college, where she is now a full-time student, that Ambika told me what happened.

"One evening my room-mate and I were preparing for bed. Saramma told me she always read a portion before retiring but this time asked me if I would like to read it. It was from John's Gospel:

> You did not choose Me but I chose you
> and appointed you to go and bear fruit -
> fruit that will last. Then the Father will give
> whatever you ask in My name..
>
> (John 15.16)

"I closed my eyes just for a second. *And then there was Jesus standing in the moonlight!* I no longer sensed Saramma there but only Him, only Jesus. She was perplexed and didn't know what was happening. I told her I could not describe the joy and peace I felt. To think I had always refused Him! But now I believed God had spoken, and oh I wanted to receive Him! I cried and cried so bitterly."

That was February 14, 1983. Ambika lost no time in telling the Jacobs, who rejoiced with her. From then on she'd read a portion from the Bible every day and it seemed that every verse was directed to her, telling her that she was ordained to go and share Christ's good news. "The trouble was," Ambika said, "I didn't have enough knowledge to discuss the Bible adequately. If anyone argued with me, I couldn't explain the truth."

One thing Ambika could do. She wanted to show by a small outward sign that she had accepted Jesus, so she removed her *bottu* from her forehead. On her next visit home, this shocked her mother and sister and brother-in-law. "What's wrong with you?" they shouted. "Do you want to look like a widow?"

Ambika tried to protest. She certainly hadn't intended to make such an issue of the *bottu*. That was only a symbol of something much deeper. She had intended to talk about her discovery of Jesus but was unable to do so because of the way they felt. She returned to work, sad and discouraged.

To her surprise, her mother came to the factory a few hours later. She had kept quiet earlier, not wanting to argue with her son-in-law, but now she wanted to make peace with her daughter. At this Ambika thought she could speak frankly: "Oh mother," she said joyously, "I am a Christian now. I can't live without Him."

Her mother was shocked. "I shouldn't have let you come here in the first place," she said bitterly. "And I should never have let you remain once you started talking about God and Jesus. Now what am I to do?"

Ambika tried to console her. "But I really can't live without Jesus anymore."

Her mother burst out, "But can you live without your family?" and cried with great sobs.

Ambika did all she could to tell her mother of Jesus' love. "If you really had that love of Jesus," her mother broke in, "you wouldn't hurt us so much."

Ambika sensed opposition ahead, and felt it important to prepare for baptism. The ceremony took place on April 1, 1984, and marked the beginning of increased harrassment within the family. Her mother was determined to settle her in marriage. Ambika agreed that if they brought a Christian to her she would be willing to marry him. But her brother-in-law proposed a Hindu boy. He was angry at her refusal to consider the young man and wrote her a letter:

> Hereafter we are dead to you. If you so much as write a letter to your sister I shall leave her at once. And if you even visit your mother we will stop going there.

Ambika was pleased to learn that her mother would not be bullied into complying with this order. "Being her mother," she said, "I cannot accept that. All of my children will be welcome in my house. I shall be mother to all."

Ambika had many sleepless nights during this period. The disapproval, anger and rejection seemed unrelenting. Once when she visited there were so many relatives in the house - brothers and sisters, in-laws and children - that the pressure seemed more than she could bear. They all seemed to unite against her, shouting, accusing. She could not be alone. When she wanted to pray she'd close herself in the bathroom. Often they'd hammer on the door so that she'd have to come out.

Sometimes she'd lose her temper in frustration and shout back. That was the worst of all. To want to show the love of Christ, and then to shout like that! "God, please control my mouth," she'd pray. "Better to be a silent witness."

Occasionally after the family's noisy recriminations, her mother softened. She'd come to the factory to see Ambika quietly and murmur: "You help the family so much, and this is how they treat you!" But publicly, her mother wouldn't dare to defend her.

For a long time there was no contact between Ambika and the sister who was so dear to her. Her sister was forbidden to see her, and they no longer visited the family home. Then Ambika got word that her sister was pregnant and 'longing to see Ambi again'. Ambika found that she was working in a certain village as a teacher. She managed to go there and after classes they slipped away for a brief and tearful reunion. Ambika's sister was so overjoyed at the meeting that she couldn't help telling her husband. But he was infuriated that she had defied him.

Even Ambika's mother turned against her for a time after the ensuing trouble. "Now you see what has happened," she said, unable to take the continued strife in the family. Ambika's brother left home, taking his wife and children away, lest his children be contaminated by the Christian influence.

After prayerful consideration Ambika resigned from the factory and joined Southern Asia Bible College to study for a Bachelor of Divinity degree. During her summer holidays she worked with the Indian Evangelical Mission for two months. It was her first experience of village evangelism and personal outreach. She joined a team visiting hospitals and going from house to house, telling villagers about the one true living God, and Jesus Christ whom He sent.

Ambika's great burden is for the prostitutes or 'priestesses' in Kali Temples. She longs to go to them with the gospel and lead them to Jesus. Recently she had a vision of these women falling down a steep cliff, and heard clearly the instruction: *You tell them.* "In God's time, I will go," Ambika told me.

Now at last Ambika and her brother have been reconciled. Some time has passed since that stormy meeting which ended in his leaving the family home. Ambika longed to see him and his children, who were very dear to her. Her mother passed on Ambika's request to him, and he agreed. "It was a wonderful visit," she told me joyously. For Ambika, it was as if the past conflicts had never been.

As we sat in the quiet chapel of her college, I asked Ambika to sing to me the song of testimony she had sung at her baptism, and she sang these words:

> I'm coming in tears to the feet
> Of Jesus asking pardon.
> I was like a prodigal son
> Who was eating the fruit

Of his sinful life.
I was away from God
Going in the way of hell.

Please save the sinner by your
grace
I'm not worthy to be your child
But please accept me
At least as your servant.

To me, no song sung on the world's stage could have
sounded more beautiful.

TEN

His most solemn salute

*Now, I ask, has the time come
at last when I may go in and
see thy face and offer thee
my silent salutation?*

Rabrindrath Tagore
Gitanjali

"You must meet the policeman Sangliana," Krickwin Marak
had told me. How glad I was for that advice!

Now a Deputy Inspector General of Police, Sangliana is
an imposing figure. He has come a long way since his
boyhood days spent, like Krickwin's wife Hmingi, in a Mizo
tribe, where his grandfather was the village priest.

"Our people were spirit worshippers," Sangliana told me.
"If someone was ill, grandfather would perform an
impressive ritual and tell the sufferer he needed to sacrifice
a chicken to the angry spirit. He would stress that the
chicken had to be taken to a certain spot outside the village,
to the tree with the hollow centre. Later on grandfather
would tell one of his sons to slip off to the tree and fetch the
chicken for their supper!

"Headhunting played an important role in the tribal
life," Sangliana explained. "The Mizo was always very keen
to get to heaven, or *Piatral* as it was called. When he got
there, if he hadn't taken heads, shot animals or had a love
affair with a girl, he would be shot full of arrows by Pawla,
the resident judge of *Piatral*. It was therefore very important
to arrive leading the spirits of slaves and animals you had
killed.

"Then toward the end of the last century a wealthy
Englishman named Mr. Arthington sponsored Welsh
missionaries to go to the Mizo tribes. They found a poor,
hardworking people, surprisingly honest in their day-to-day
lives. The missionaries set to work learning the language

and making an alphabet. Then they translated the Bible and hymns, and taught the tribespeople to read and write. Within forty years, the Mizos found in the message of Jesus a wonderful alternative to spirit worship. No demon possession was heard of for a long time," Sangliana told me.

Some years earlier, in January 1871, a British tea garden manager by the name of Mr. Winchester had been killed by Mizos and his daughter kidnapped - though she was later recovered by British soldiers. Twenty-three years ago, the Mizo Christians held a service of atonement to show their repentance. In a moving ceremony, they pledged to hunt for souls instead of heads. Mizoran became the only Christian state in India, with the second highest literacy rate and a flourishing economy. Sadly, in more recent days, elements of greed and materialism have crept in: some of the teenagers are beginning to rebel, drugs are used and the Christian faith of many has become nominal. Even evil spirits are returning and demon-possession is seen once again in areas where there was none at all for many years.

Sangliana's own father was a nominal Christian, so he was not given good religious guidance as a boy. His father worked for the government, attending British officers. He used to drink country liquor and suffered from disturbing dreams. Perhaps this was due to his sorrow at losing his wife when Sangliana was a boy of five. The widower cried many days and nights after that, and was only stopped by relatives from killing his four children and himself in an effort to be reconciled with his departed wife.

Later they moved to a northern part of Mizoram. Sangliana recalls the boys running around without clothing, and the joke that they had one pair of trousers which they'd use in turn. He was in the village school until the third standard when the costs became prohibitive to his impoverished father, who decided to send him off to an uncle. Sangliana walked the one hundred and fifteen miles without shoes - then found he had to walk twelve miles each way to school every day.

In 1957 Sangliana was sent to a Bengali High School in Imphal. He was very happy there, living in a hut with a mud floor and making do on very little.

Sangliana completed his schooling in Manipur, increasingly aware of the obstacles in his life. His health was not good, and he often studied up to thirteen hours a day, realising that with indifferent health he'd need good qualifications to be of value to an employer. His sisters and younger brother needed an education, too, and he'd have to help. Then his father remarried and began another family. In time there were six more children! Sangliana, now at university, felt his own responsibilities increasing.

His father was frequently ill now, and in and out of hospitals with head pains. It was later found that he had a tumour, and he died just too soon to see his son obtain an honours degree in Economics.

Two years before, Sangliana had reached a crisis point, wondering where he was going in life. This was resolved once and forever when he took the step of commitment to Jesus, making Him his Saviour and Lord.

Even as a new Christian in College, Sangliana wanted to tell people about Jesus. He sometimes went to hospitals and prayed with sick people. One such encounter seemed to be a foretaste of what would often happen later on. The patient, a forty-five year old Mizo lady, terrified the nurses with her unpredictable hysterical behaviour. Sangliana went over to her as she was having one of her 'fits', and started to tell her about Jesus. She told him a powerful spirit was working on her. Sometimes he would come in and tell her she was like a lizard crawling on the wall and would never get to heaven. As Sangliana began to speak, the spirit rushed to enter him. Pressure formed within his head and it seemed that his head was swelling and about to explode! He rushed from the place and ran all the way to his hostel, his head still throbbing.

It was a horrific experience for a young Christian but it left him in no doubt about the forces of evil and the vulnerability of unbelievers when these forces were released. Sangliana learned that the woman's behaviour had changed after a seance of sorts with two *Sadhus* who took certain leaves and bound them to her wrists to 'help' her. At first she felt wonderful and there were no problems anywhere. But soon disturbing things began to happen: her children were burnt with 'flying' cigarette ends, and someone other than herself took over her body, tearing her apart.

Sangliana prayed about her and other troubled people like her, who desperately needed the help of the Saviour. If only he could be an evangelist! He prayed fervently, wanting to work for Christ's kingdom but knowing there were many in his family who were his responsibility now. "Lord," he said finally, "in whatever position you put me, *please use me*!"

There was an All-Indian competitive exam for the selection of officers for the Indian Civil Service. Sangliana read the poster carefully and thought he might apply. After all, there was no one to support him for his post-graduate studies. He'd never thought about the police before. "I really wasn't a fit person to be a policeman," he told me with a twinkle in his eye. "I didn't have whiskers on my face, or a round belly or a fierce look!"

But after taking the exam, he was offered a place in the Indian Police Service. He took it, thinking that it might be a stepping stone for a future career. And then he was sent to the National Police Academy at Mount Abu for training. He also became an Anglican lay reader, believing this was a vital part of his Christian duty.

Some months after the start of his training programme, he thought about the officers over him, and how he saluted them each day. A new desire came to him. On his first day off, he called an orderly and asked him to press his full, best uniform. He arranged for the watchman to open the church and stand guard. He put on his uniform, and checked everything carefully. It had to be perfect.

He went in to the church, alone, and stood before the altar at attention. "God," he said, "I have come to give You my most solemn salute! I don't know whether I'll fit in to this life, and whether this is where You want me. Just please keep my life and future in Your hands."

And he gave Him the very best salute he could give.

Sangliana was posted to Bangalore in 1968. At the same

time he knew he had to get involved in Christian work. Whenever he received posting orders he'd pray: "Go before me and speak to the people; prepare the way so that I can work for You."

He was sent to Assam in 1971, commanding a paramilitary battalion, to settle a law and order situation. One night a Bengali Hindu constable was brought to his bungalow under armed escort. He was thrashing around, breathing in gasps and lunging about. There was a terrifying look in his eyes.

"The first thing I had to do was pray," Sangliana told me. "I knew that I'd have to call on the Hindu priests first of all, to give them a chance to help him. But I already had the conviction that it would be up to Jesus to deliver him, and no one else. Nevertheless I decided to have him locked up and let them see if they could help." During that week three Hindu priests arrived and tried various rituals to cast out the evil spirit. One said, "This is the toughest case I have ever faced." He couldn't do anything for the man and left. Others came but they too were unable to help.

Sangliana told his commander to bring the man under escort. He told his wife, Rovi, what he planned to do: he was going to keep the man in their guest room and pray for him, and God was going to work!

The man was brought in and the orderly stood by the door, watching. Sangliana came in holding his Bible. He faced the man and said, "I command you to go."

"I will not go!" came from the man.

"I command you to go in the name of Jesus," Sangliana repeated. The man lunged forward as if to attack him, but Sangliana had been holding his Bible in front of him. It acted as a shield when the man grabbed him. At that moment the man fell down, unconscious. Sangliana and the orderly watched in silence as he slowly got to his feet, totally calm, normal and free. The man couldn't recall what happened. "I don't know why I'm here," he said. Even the memory of it had left him

The same night Sangliana explained what had happened. "Would you please say thank you to Jesus?" he advised. "If you want to stay free of these things, you must give your life to Him." He presented a Bengali Bible to the constable, who received it with thanks.

A week later Sangliana was presented with a new crisis. A son of one of his battalion tailors was possessed by an evil spirit. His father requested that the chief of the village come and repeat *mantras* to deliver him. When this had no effect Sangliana came to pray for him. He knelt down, pressing his Bible on the boy's chest. "Here is another case for You," Sangliana prayed, "please glorify Your name!" Just as before, the boy seemed to crumple on the floor and lay still, unconscious. And when he awoke, he had no recollection of what had happened!

A month later Sangliana was transferred back to Bangalore. He returned in charge of a district as Superintendent of Police. There were ceremonies and tributes, and he found himself honoured and garlanded. "Thank you for this garland," he prayed silently. "I receive this only because of You."

On one occasion a young man came from a nearby village to report an assault and Sangliana received the complaint. The youth said that the villagers had turned on him because he criticised the priest. Apparently the priest was the owner of a powerful (and prosperous) 'deity' who, he claimed, could understand all languages and answer questions. It was a very heavy god, he explained, because of all the food villagers gave to it. Four assistants (friends of the priest) were needed to hold it and stop it toppling on the worshippers! When a question was asked it, it would push its carriers forward if the answer was 'yes' and backward if the answer was 'no'. There was always a steady stream of people willing to serve food to the god and have their questions answered.

Sangliana and a Christian friend went to the village to investigate. "I'm told you have a very powerful god here," Sangliana said. "May I see it?" Reluctantly the priest opened up a small room in his house, and there was the image, a wooden figure with a colourful face and feminine features. His four henchmen held on to it protectively. Sangliana watched them carefully and invited the villagers to ask questions of the deity, while warning the henchmen they would risk serious action if they attempted to move it. This time it never moved.

Sangliana took out his Bible and held it in front of him. "I believe the priest has been eating your animals," he told the people. This god cannot answer your questions." In that village twenty-five people became Christians that year. And the 'god' was completely abandoned by the villagers.

Wrestling with the devil was not always as easy as that. One day Sangliana was confronted with a very tall strong fellow who had an evil spirit. He persuaded the man to come into the bungalow. Sangliana knelt down with the Bible pressed against the man's heart. The man went into a rage and they began to struggle. He had terrifying power, coming toward Sangliana and trying to pin him down like a wrestler whilst calling on his god Venkateswara. The struggle went on, with Sangliana praying and resisting with all his strength. "God! Interfere now!" Sangliana shouted out. "If you don't it will humiliate all of us who believe in You! It is You who are the true God, is it not?"

Finally the man collapsed, overcome by the Spirit of the true God. When he opened his eyes, he was free. Sangliana sat with him quietly and opened the Bible, wanting to show him how to approach God for help. The man could hardly read and so Sangliana had to explain it. One month later, Sangliana reported happily, the man was avidly reading the Bible for himself!

In December 1980, there was a very frightening case in a village involving a poor woman who had been demon possessed for many years. Sangliana set out to visit her. When he arrived, he asked the villagers, "You have been praying to your gods about this for a long time and they have not answered. If mine hears, will you believe in Him?"

He went into the woman's thatched hut and knelt down on the mud floor. He commanded the spirit to leave her in Jesus' name. Within two minutes the devil left her. Some enthusiastic villagers hastened away and returned with yet another woman possessed by an evil spirit. Sangliana prayed,

"God thank You for that but please will You act quickly?" The spirit left her at once. It didn't have a chance to struggle. Sangliana turned to the amazed villagers. "It is Jesus my God who should be worshipped!" he said. And some believed that day.

That evening Sangliana was speaking at a college Student Union function. He gave this account of the two women who were delivered. There were some reporters there who listened and took notes. Shortly after, an article appeared in a State-wide newspaper. The following week there was an Assembly session, and a legislator rose and put a request to the Chief Minister: "A Senior Police Officer has been involved in some prayer ceremonies with villagers said to be demon possessed. Would you investigate this please and make your report available?"

Sangliana was delighted to describe the event in full, giving the names of those who were delivered, and the many eye witnesses to the healing. It was a six-page report and ended with his comment: "I firmly believe that all the incidents which are recorded in the Bible are true." The report was read carefully in the Assembly by the legislators and ministers.

Sangliana enjoyed relating these incidents to me, but it was a pleasure combined with amazement that God should use 'a sinner like me'. "I just run around in my humble way," he said, and meant it.

ELEVEN

Hebron

*When I was yet a Sikh, God seemed
so very, very far away - but now I can
say, He is so near! I know that His life is
flowing through me!*

Bakht Singh

The population of Hyderabad must be the most literate in India, I decided with amusement, studying the slogans on nearly every wall. Even new houses prove an irresistible surface to the slogan writers and long before the finish is put on many new buildings, the walls are festooned with red or blue lettering, each figure several feet high. And once a slogan is scrawled on a wall, it's there to stay. Even a political notice from previous elections is safe for posterity. No one would dream of erasing it by painting the wall!

But surely Osmania University deserves a special prize for the most lavishly decorated walls and buildings. In such collegiate areas, the themes are often political:

LIFT THE POLICE CAMPS FROM THE COLLEGES
DOWN WITH COMMERCIALISATION OF   EDUCATION
SYSTEM
LONG LIVE P D S U

In the centre of the city, wall slogans take on a more general theme:

DOWN WITH DOWRY
DR JATHANAND FOR V D, SEX, PILES, SKIN

And often, on billboards and telegraph poles, Christian posters announce:

COME CLAP WITH THE GOSPELLERS
CHRISTIAN SPIRITUAL MEETINGS
SCHOOL OF THE SPIRIT
HEALING PRAYERS

But the most beautiful notices of all are seen over a several mile stretch from the airport to the approach of the city. Bible verses in English, Telegu and Hindi are superbly painted in red, blue and gold, proclaiming messages such as:

JESUS SAYS, LOOK UNTO ME
AND BE YE SAVED ALL THE ENDS OF THE EARTH

I looked out of the window and saw yet another beautifully painted Scripture text:

FOR GOD SO LOVED THE WORLD
THAT HE GAVE HIS ONLY BEGOTTEN SON
THAT WHOSOEVER BELIEVETH IN HIM...

"Who paints those Bible messages?" I asked my companion. "Is it someone you know?"

"It's some fellow who travels around. He comes here, paints some more walls, and then we don't see him again for a year or so. He travels to villages and cities, painting his verses anywhere he can."

"Do you think I could get to meet him" I asked. "I'd love to know who he is and who he works for!"

"I believe he does it himself," was the reply. "Just an itinerant sign-writer."

"No, an artist," I thought, "doing more with his talents than most artists do, however highly praised." I hoped I would get the chance to meet this servant of Christ.

My main reason for being in Hyderabad this time, however, was to visit Hebron, the home of Bakht Singh. I was also looking forward to meeting my doctor friend Sudershan again.

It was really through Sudershan that my love for India

began. When, as a young college student, he had written to
a Christian radio programme in England asking for a pen-
pal, I had been the one to pick up his card. We had
corresponded for some years before I had ever had the
chance to visit India and finally meet him.

Now we were on our way to Hebron, where the annual
Holy Convocation meetings were being held. Over twenty
thousand Christians come to Hebron at this time, from all
over the country.

We passed dozens of hired buses, church coaches with
their names written on the sides and vans with Bible verses
all over them. And the crowds: more than I'd ever seen
before, even in India. Thousands of men in white flanked
one side of the road, and an equal amount of women and
children the other. There were some well-dressed women in
silk sarees but many more simple village women in home-
spun material. An endless stream moved in and out of the
tiny openings into the two tents. One vast *shamiana* seating
five thousand was for the women. This was linked via the
platform with a similar one for men. A service was in
progress but there was as much quiet socialising inside the
tents as in the road. Anyway the meeting, like all others,
would go on for hours.

I first met Bakht Singh when I was an undergraduate in
New York in the 1950's. He came to speak to us in chapel
and his words were powerful and penetrating: "I didn't
come to America to ask for money. You Americans want
money; not I. God meets my needs..."

Bakht Singh sometimes relates the story of the time when
he was a boy at school, staying in a hostel. One day his
father came to see him. "He was an old-fashioned man with
a very big turban and a long *vashti*, and wearing country
shoes. He brought me ghee and sweets and gave me
money."

But his friends were watching, and young Bakht was
embarrassed. When a classmate asked who the man was, his
son replied that he was "just an old man from our village."

"I took my father's money and everything he brought,"

Brother Bakht said later, "but was ashamed to confess him as my father." He used this illustration to show how mankind is ready to take God's gifts of life and care, without giving Him the love and devotion He deserves. But he also told the story against himself to show his own ingratitude to the Father and how he denied Him for so many years.

As he grew up in the Punjab, Bakht Singh became a militant member of the community, exhibiting fierce pride in the Sikh religion and bitter hatred for 'foreign' faiths. Christianity, in particular, became the object of his wrath. One night in 1919 he tore up the Bible to show his hatred for it and for Christians, and went on to blaspheme against God and the followers of Christ. At the same time he began to live an evil life, rebelling against God and His holy laws for many years. But it was the love and mercy of God that exposed his sins, not harsh condemnation or judgment. "He Himself came to me," Brother Bakht wrote later. "I never went to Him. For I was, in fact, going away from Him."

Finally on December 16, 1929 while alone in his room he heard these words:

> This is my body broken for you; this is my
> blood of the New Testament shed for the
> remission of your sins.

That morning his life was turned around. The cultured rogue became a confessing sinner and a cleansed child of God!

Some months later a Christian seized his hand and asked him: "Brother, why don't you go back and preach in India?" Bakht Singh's defences went up. First of all, he informed the well-meaning man, he was an engineer, and it had taken him years of study to get there. Secondly, he was the victim of a nervous stammer. He couldn't possibly stand up before a crowd of people and talk!

For two years Bakht Singh wrestled with this suggestion. He tried to persuade God that he could give money to support others, or build buildings. But always the words returned to him:

I do not want your money. I want you.

Bakht Singh returned to India in 1933. In Bombay he met his parents, who told him that he could not return to his home in the Punjab unless he promised not to tell anyone he was a Christian.

He said later: "If I had come back to India as a drunkard and adulterer, they would have welcomed me. Now that the Lord had changed me and given me a new life, they did not want me!" He had to say, "I am sorry; my Lord comes first."

Several years later they again met at a railway station. His father told him, "You can read the Bible and pray; you can do anything else that you like; but do not say that you are a Christian in your home town. When you are away, however, you are free to do as you wish."

He replied: "Father, the Lord Jesus is my life; how can I live if I deny Him?"

I sat with Brother Bakht Singh and Brother T.E. Koshy discussing the way God has led them and met their needs through the years. "Some years ago," Brother Koshy said, "there was a church growth study made. It was discovered that our believers' assemblies were the fastest-growing Christian group in India. We were asked: 'What is your strategy? What is your methodology?'

"Our answer was and is this," he said. "It is prayer, and a willingness to be led by the Holy Spirit. It is three-fold submission to Jesus Christ: His Headship; His Lordship; His Kingship."

"It is being led His way," said Brother Bakht, "and not man's." Because of this, the believers' emphasis is on the Word of God, believing that the New Testament pattern for living can be applied to *any* culture.

The believers' assemblies now number over six hundred in India itself, with others in surrounding areas. "We have four hundred full-time workers," Brother Koshy told me, "with the largest concentration in Andhra Pardesh. But there's no membership, no counting heads," he smiled, "so we have no hold on anyone."

Brother Samuel joined us, a big kindly-faced fellow who

was in charge of the food all week. I thought that if this had been a secular convention, the Catering Manager would have been a nervous wreck by now! But not Brother Samuel. He was calmly telling me that they fed "somewhere between twenty and twenty-five thousand yesterday." He said cheerfully that they fed as many as twenty-one thousand in one meal, but that they averaged fifteen thousand most days that week. This meant one hundred kilograms of rice each day, to say nothing of fifty thousand gallons of water to prepare it!

"Each year the costs for the Holy Convocation are met by the believers," said Brother Koshy. "We don't owe any man anything. This year it cost about five hundred thousand Rs. And everything has been paid."

I looked up to see a long queue of people silently and patiently waiting to see Brother Bakht. It was time to go. He leaned forward and prayed for me, for my life and family, for whatever work God had for me.

I remembered the dynamic preacher of thirty years before. He was an old man now, in his eighties, but his spirit was as strong as ever:

> I have been young, and now am old; yet
> have I not seen the righteous forsaken nor
> his seed begging bread.

> (Ps. 37:25)

TWELVE

A prisoner for her faith

*Let only that little of my
fetters be left whereby I
am bound with Thy will, and
Thy purpose is carried out in
my life - and that is the fetter
of Thy love.*

Rabrindrath Tagore
Gitanjali

It was the death of a leading politician that set Esther Chitra thinking. "Where will his soul go?" she wondered. "How futile life and achievements seem if all ends at the grave!" She was walking along the road and saw a crumpled leaflet. Normally she would not have noticed, but something made her pick it up. She smoothed it out and read:

> What good will it be for a man, if he gains
> the whole world, yet forfeits his soul? Or
> what can a man give in exchange for his
> soul?

> (Matthew 16:26)

The writer spoke of an after-life, and the need to decide for God here and now. She realised that this was the Christian answer to all her questions.

And so began a journey of faith that was one day to take her to Hebron. It was there, some years later, that I met Esther and heard her story.

Until that day Esther had scorned the idea that Jesus Christ might be the living God. Like other children of well-educated Indians, she had been sent by her doctor father to a convent school in Madras City. Here she received teaching of a high quality, was encouraged to have a high moral standard, but learnt nothing about the Lord Jesus Christ.

However, after the incident of the leaflet a Christian classmate gave her a book, the life of Sadhu Sundar Singh. Here she read with growing fascination how Jesus Christ actually met with an individual and entered his life in a personal way. "How was it," she wondered, "that only Jesus appeared to Sundar Singh when he was on the brink of suicide? Why were the Hindu gods not there to help him?"

In the weeks that followed Esther found herself deeply involved in a search for the truth: was God the Hindu god? the Muslim one? or was Jesus Christ God? She longed to know the True God.

Her search went on during her Medical studies in Kurnoul, Andhra Pradesh. One night, after her studies, she took down a Bible she had been given.. With a strong impression that God was about to speak, she opened it to the Book of Isaiah, and her eyes fell on these words:

> This is like the days of Noah when I swore
> that the waters of Noah would never again
> cover the earth. So now I have sworn not
> to be angry with you, never to rebuke you
> again, though the mountains be shaken
> and the hills be removed, yet my unfailing
> love for you will not be shaken nor my
> covenant of peace be removed, says the
> Lord who has compassion on you.
>
> (Isa. 54:9-10)

"To think of such a mighty God making a covenant of peace with man! That is unheard of in Hinduism," she thought. Then she knew clearly in her heart that Christ was God. It was 11.30 p.m. when she knelt down. "You are the only true and living God in this world," she prayed. And at once a heavenly joy rushed into her heart like a flood. Esther sensed a Person standing beside her, with a presence more powerful than the most charismatic human personality.

"Do not be afraid, I will be with you," He was saying.

Esther had struggled with fears for many years: fears of death, of catastrophe or evil happening to herself or her family. Now she realised God was telling her, "If you died now, you would be with Me." The very worst thing that could happen - death - would be life's supreme joy: to be in the presence of the living God. So the believer need never fear again! At that moment she was enveloped by a wonderful peace, and all the fears were gone. Another sensation came to her in those first few moments of spiritual transformation. It was a sense of cleansing. She could only describe it as "something washing my heart of all my sins until it was clean and pure."

If this peace and cleansing came as a complete surprise, she was to experience even more changes in the days to come. The following morning she was about to make a small excuse to a friend. Just a tiny, insignificant lie. Suddenly she thought: "This small, 'harmless' lie is sin in His sight." Without uttering the untruth, she turned and went away.

That same day she'd made plans to see a film. As she prepared to go, the words came to her clearly:

> I have cleansed your heart. Why see evil on
> the screen? The joy I give you is complete.
> You need not see the counterfeit.

Attending films and reading novels had been Esther's great love. It was a wonderful way to relax after long hours of study. But within days she found these diversions no longer interested her. She did not consciously 'deny' herself: their attraction simply disappeared. A student would not speak to her: they had clashed and quarrelled, and then gone their separate ways. Now God said, "Go and make peace" and Esther did so. And more than that: she went with great joy and told her about the love of Jesus!

From that first night in the hostel, God began to teach her by renewing her mind, by changing the affections of her heart. "Look at that wall," she felt He was saying. "It has no life. And yet you have worshipped lifeless statues and pictures. If you asked the wall anything, could it answer you? In a similar way, how could the pictures answer? So why worship them?" Esther marvelled at this revelation.

She looked at her face in the mirror. Lifting her hand to the *bottu*, her caste mark, she took it off. No one told her to do this, but now it seemed out of place. What did the *bottu* have to do with her? Now the living God was protecting her, not Shiva! But that simple act heralded a furore in the hostel. As long as her spiritual discoveries remained within her heart, no one could quarrel with them. But as soon as she took off the mark, she was making a statement to the world outside. Angry words were spoken. The principal heard what she had done and threatened her. Her professor gave her an ultimatum: "Don't come in to my class without your caste mark!"

Esther was distressed at the implications of this. If she could not attend that class, it would be impossible to carry on her medical studies. She turned to the Lord and asked for help. In her reading, she received His reply:

> Stop trusting in man, who has but a breath
> in his nostrils. Of what account is he?
>
> (Isa. 2:22)

"Thank you, Lord," she prayed. "Then I'll not go to class." Amazingly, a strike broke out in the college the following day and it was forced to close indefinitely! It was about that time that Esther first visited Hebron. "That was an oasis for me," she was to tell me later. "It was a wonderful experience at that time to enjoy love and fellowship with other believers, and to join them in studying the Word of God."

For Esther, though, the crisis had not passed. Her professor wrote to Esther's parents to complain of her behaviour. She too felt it right to send them a letter and tell them what had happened. The two letters brought swift action. Esther's father came for her at once, and took her back to Madras. She was effectively cut off from all Christian contacts, and with her studies now discontinued, she remained a prisoner in the house for one and a half years.

Her mother burnt her Bible and the only thing that remained to her was prayer. She prayed in the bathroom and in her bedroom but opportunities for privacy were few.

And it was like being imprisoned without trial: she had no idea how soon she would be released.

In time her parents allowed her to return to her studies. But she was required to stay with her grandmother, to prevent her from associating with the Christian believers. Esther completed her training and returned to Madras where she obtained a medical post with Madras Corporation. This was the start of a seven year period spent in complete isolation from other Christians. She was permitted to attend work, but required to return home immediately afterwards. Her freedom, apart from the hours spent at the dispensary, was totally restricted. In the early days, when she attempted to go to a meeting, the doors were locked to keep her in. All those years her wages were taken from her, to increase her dependence on the family. She could not see or communicate with any of her believing friends.

Esther was very conscious, though, of God's hand in her circumstances. She felt no licence from the Lord to disobey, knowing that no man could require anything of her unless God permitted it. And as the months turned into years, she sensed that it was God - not man - who kept her in that place to teach her about Himself and to lead her to a sanctified life.

Some of these lessons were severe ones. She was forced to rely utterly on the Lord Jesus Christ. She obtained a Bible and hid it, but it was discovered and destroyed. The same happened to a second, and a third one. Her only source of strength was God alone.

All that time, many people at Hebron were fasting and praying for Esther. And quite suddenly, her release came. One day she knew that at last God had given her the liberty to leave the family home. She received this with great joy, but there was still the problem of where to go. And since she was penniless, how would she manage?

Then the Lord spoke to her clearly. *Go to Hebron.* It was not what she expected. She had assumed that the most likely solution would be to take shelter at *Jeho'shama* in Madras, the fellowship house of Assembly believers. That way she could continue her work with the Corporation. But God said: *Go to Hebron*. That meant an expensive journey from Madras to Hyderabad. Esther could not doubt the Lord's provision, but she wondered how this would be done.

The following morning she arose as usual and prepared for work. Unexpectedly, her wages arrived and for the first time in all those years, her parents were not there to intercept them. Esther took her cheque and a few possessions and left the house. She went to the bank and cashed the cheque, and then boarded the bus to Hyderabad. She was free at last, at the age of thirty.

THIRTEEN

Do you know who you are worshipping?

Whom dost thou worship in the
lonely dark corner of a temple
with doors all shut?
Open thine eyes and see thy God
is not before thee!

Rabindrath Tagore
Gitanjali

Every day multitudes pass through the gates of Hyderabad on their way to work, struggling to support their families, trying to find happiness or entertainment. Day after day, many enter mosques and temples throughout the city, seeking blessings from their gods. But for all their pujas and pilgrimages, sacrifices and rituals, the gods of wood and stone cannot hear or answer their cries.

Fourteen years ago Samuel John Babu was one face among those millions. Once respected in his community as a police sub-inspector, and looked up to by his wife and eight children, his life was now wrecked by alcoholism, liver disease and high blood pressure. The doctor predicted he had not long to live.

One afternoon in December 1972, seeking to salvage something from his uncertain life, he wearily climbed the steps of the temple and stood before the god.

Suddenly it was as if an electric shock surged through his body, and he became aware of a strange and wonderful Presence beside him. In that moment he found himself speaking with an unseen Being.

"Do you know who you're worshipping?" asked the unseen Voice.

"Who am I worshipping?" John stammered.

"You left the living God and are worshipping a dead

god!" the Being said.

"Who is the living God?" was all John could ask.

"Jesus Christ."

John immediately turned away from the image and walked out of the temple. He sank onto a cement bench at the foot of the steps, overwhelmed with this Presence. Immediately the Lord began to speak again:

"You have been praying for many things: your career, a secure future, and all the hopes and plans of your life. You have been forsaken by friends and relatives, and rejected by the world. Now you are nearing death."

"What will happen when I die?" was all John could ask.

"You are on your way to hell - an eternal lake of fire. But even though you were rejected by everyone," the Lord said, "I have come in search of you, to save you."

"What shall I do, Lord?" John cried. "I've made such a mess of my life! How could it be possible to come to You?" and he began weeping, forgetting all around him, conscious only of his miserable, sinful life. He did not know what to do!

Jesus said: "Believe in Me; I'll save you."

John drifted home, as he put it, still with the wonderful Presence of God all round him. His wife, eldest son and eldest daughter were there to greet him and looked up amazed. They too felt the Spirit of God in that room. And they could see that something awesome had happened. That evening John prayed to the living God for the first time in his home. He asked Him for help and guidance, and felt a tremendous peace in his heart. And that night his wife, son and daughter surrendered their lives, with John's, to the living Lord and Saviour Jesus Christ.

In the early hours of the next morning, John heard God's voice again. He called out, "My son!" and told John, "I am calling you for My ministry."

John protested, "Lord, I don't know anything about the Bible! How can I possibly serve You in this way?"

But Jesus said, "Submit yourself to Me, and I will use you to establish many churches and assemblies, and do many things with your life." And He began to speak to John about these things. The next day, John was miraculously led by the Lord to a Spirit-filled pastor who began to instruct and care for him. And on 10 February, 1973 in Nizamabad, John and his wife, his eldest son and daughter, obeyed the Lord and were all baptised in water.

"It was years later," he told me as we sat in the shady porch of his home in the Parsi Gutte section of Hyderabad, "that I learnt the circumstances of my birth. My mother could have no children and so my parents adopted a boy. But one day a Christian evangelist came to our district, and my mother asked him to pray for her, that she might have a child. She promised that if God would grant her this, she would give him back to God. So when I was born, she called me Samuel John. But I never knew that I was marked for God. My parents died when I was young and it was not until six years after becoming a Christian that I learnt how God had His hand upon my life all along."

Completely delivered from the craving for drink, John's health was wonderfully restored. Then the Lord gave him a new job in clerical work. He continued in this for several years, attending the church where he was first ministered to, studying the Bible, and learning about the goodness and provision of God. Later on God spoke to him about becoming a preacher, and directed John and his family to Armoor, a hostile part of Andhra Pradesh. At first John didn't want to go there. How would they receive them? Would his family come to any harm? But then he realised he would have to trust God in this, too. With the family joining him in believing God for every need, they moved to Armoor.

It turned out to be a great blessing. It was there John was able to lead his first men and women to Jesus Christ. There he saw the first miracles among the people - which are still evident today. The church saw blind restored to sight and many other healings from God's hand. "I vividly recall one man in those early days," smiled John, "suffering from TB of the spinal cord. The doctors at the hospital where he lay said that he would die within fifteen days. Friends took him from the hospital and brought him to the church. He was prayed for, and Jesus healed him totally. He is strong and healthy today and serving Jesus Christ."

The church in Armoor began to thrive, with many Hindus coming to faith in Jesus as their living Lord. In time the work there multiplied to such an extent that there are now eight fellowships instead of one, and each month new Hindu converts are added to the churches there.

"In 1980 God spoke to me about returning to Hyderabad to begin a work here," John continued. "But by now we were so happy in Armoor and the work was going so well, that we didn't want to leave. Nevertheless we knew the faithfulness of God in all things. We recalled how reluctant we were to go to Armoor in the first place - and yet He had met our every need. Would He not also supply these things if we returned to Hyderabad?"

And so John and his family went back to the city where they lived before Jesus Christ came into their lives.

"In the past four years at Sion fellowship," John told me, "we have seen Hindus from all walks of life come to Jesus Christ: businessmen, teachers, illiterate village folk, students. All kinds of people! And then they work together: some teach the village people how to read. Some of the unemployed are taught skills so that they can have a trade. Above all, we are learning to love each other in Jesus Christ, and to live together.

"In our fellowship, the hall is no longer big enough to hold all who attend. We are building a prayer hall to seat a thousand, and we know that God will fill it. The work has spread throughout Andhra Pradesh and there are now forty centres within the fellowship, including eleven in Hyderabad and eight in Armoor. Most of these are self-supporting - and they themselves support Christian workers and missionaries. And every month, we see thirty to thirty-five Hindus discovering that they can know Jesus Christ personally and have a new life in Him."

One such was Chintakindu Ananthaiah, a big, tall man in long shirt and *dhoti*, who came up and quietly joined us on the porch. Fifty-eight year old 'Anan' was from the Komati community, a businessman dealing in grain and pulses. He was a member of the Vaishya caste, whose father had been a seller of foodstuffs in Hyderabad.

Anan had had severe stomach trouble for about fifteen years, and been operated on several times but found no relief. He suffered from an ulcer, and also related abdominal problems. Of course the more he worried about his ailments, the more his health deteriorated. He spent time and money going from doctor to doctor, but this did not help. Anan also sought relief through many *pujas* and prayers. Even as a boy he was very religious and exacting in the performance of his Hindu rituals. Surely the gods would grant him healing, he reasoned, if he prayed enough.

It wasn't just his own health that caused him anxiety - his wife was sick too. And how would he continue working when he was ill all the time? What would happen to his home? And then, as if that wasn't enough, his daughter began to associate and pray with Christians! His whole world seemed to be crumbling. Small wonder that lately he couldn't eat properly, and when he did eat, he couldn't digest it...

"Father, please let my friends pray with you," his daughter pleaded with him. "Your *pujas* haven't done you any good, have they?"

But Anan insulted the friends she brought to help him. Some days later he was feverish, too ill to get up, and back they came! This time he was too sick to protest, and they gathered round him and prayed.

Surprisingly enough, his health improved somewhat after this and he began to eat slowly. Gradually he got his strength back and within a fortnight he agreed to visit Sion Fellowship where his daughter had started to attend. That night, there were special prayers for the sick and he went up to be prayed for.

To his great amazement, Anan lost all pain and sickness. He began to eat heartily, as in days gone by - he was beginning to feel normal again!

During the Hindu festival, there were celebrations and *pujas*. Anan returned to the temple, to the prayers and ceremonies he knew best. After all, this was the way he had always worshipped. It was the most familiar to him. But almost immediately he suffered a set-back and was attacked by the old pains. Just when he thought he was healed! He had difficulty eating and sleeping. His daughter pleaded, "Go back to Sion, and let John Babu pray with you again."

This time Anan followed her suggestion. He asked Brother John to pray with him, and he did. But he also told a surprised Anan, "You lost your healing because you returned to the *pujas* and prayed to the idols."

Anan at once recognised that this was the truth. He repented of what he had done, and prayed for forgiveness. Even as he went home he knew he was healed; permanently. He went into his house and took down all the gods from his shelves.

In a dream Anan saw Jesus beckoning him to cross a river and come to Him on the other side. Anan knew that this meant God wanted him to be baptised. Without delay he went to John Babu and told him. His daughter received the news with joy. Anan was baptised in 1983. Shortly afterwards, four other members of the *Vaishya* community became believers in Jesus Christ.

But Anan's wife was less than pleased, and for a time their relationship was strained. His business had suffered, too, during his illness and when he first became a Christian. He had been forced to borrow money to meet other expenses, and then these new debts loomed.

Nevertheless God had not only healed Anan's stomach and digestive system, He had healed Anan's *worry*. When problems were put before him, Anan knew what to do now. He could pray to Jesus who said:

> Who of you by worrying can add a single
> hour to his life?.....
> And do not set your heart on what you will
> eat or drink. Do not worry about it.....
> But seek His kingdom, and these things will
> be given to you as well.
>
> (Luke 12:25, 29, 31)

Anan began to listen to Christian songs on the radio, and sing along with them. It gave him a new lift to his spirit, and his wife listened too when she was doing her chores.

John Babu told me, "Anan used to be a typical Komati businessman: rough-speaking and driving a hard bargain. And if you didn't pay your bills, look out! He could shout angrily and harrass a debtor as good as the next one.

"Now, even though many people owe him money, he's very gentle with them. At church conventions, with perhaps a thousand people, Aran handles all the supplies."

Anan and John and others are praying about starting a co-operative, but they want to make sure that it's God's timing.

"Please pray for my wife," Anan asked me shyly, "that she will come to follow Jesus too. Then we shall be able to work for Him together."

FOURTEEN

Many members, one body

Now you are the body of Christ,
and each one of you is a part of it.

1 Cor. 12:27

Raju and I sat in a restaurant having a favourite Hyderabad dish, chicken *biryani*. It was delicious. A friend of Sudershan's, Raju often acted as guide and translator for me.

Raju works as a librarian at an institute of technology, but his special love and calling is his personal evangelism ministry, which he calls 'sowing seeds'. He considers himself privileged to earn one thousand seven hundred Rs a month. From that he is able to rent two rooms, one for his sister and one for himself, and also purchase tracts, booklets and other supplies for door-to-door visitation. He writes off to Christian organisations in the U.S. and U.K. who offer free literature. Other supplies he purchases himself. He can be seen regularly in various areas, distributing the appropriate literature to each language group. Sometimes he is even able to furnish tracts to local church workers from his supplies.

Such effort is the result of a very deep love for the Lord Jesus Christ. It certainly shines from his face. You don't have to be in his presence for long to know where he has set his affections.

Raju comes from the village of Nallagandla, sixteen miles outside Hyderabad. His family was one of many poor ones in the village who earned their livelihood from the seasonal production and sale of fruits. Raju lived in a typical white-washed mud house with his parents and six sisters. "The Lord caught my attention at a very young age, like Samuel in the Bible," Raju told me humbly. "I was very zealous and interested in religion and loved to hear the stories of Jesus. Even at an early age I took Bible correspondence courses and was hungry to learn more."

Raju's father had a deep spiritual experience as a teenager and lived zealously for Jesus for the remainder of his life. No doubt his godly walk influenced his young son. When Raju was just fourteen, his father died, but a few months later Raju committed his life to Christ. At once he developed a keen interest in spreading the gospel through Christian literature and through personal house-to-house contacts.

Raju went to Osmania University and obtained degrees in Public Administration, Economics, Library Science and Divinity. "Why do you Indians want so many degrees?" I teased him.

"It's a question of income," he explained to me patiently. "Before I obtained my first degree, I was making three hundred Rs. a month. After my first degree I made four hundred and twenty-five Rs. a month. My salary has gradually increased until now I earn one thousand seven hundred."

Raju told me about a Christian college where he worked as a librarian for three years. He didn't really want to go there but the officials were very keen for him to come. The pay was very poor, five hundred Rs. per month, and Raju felt that if he took secular employment he could make much more money and support himself in his own literature distribution work. Nevertheless he was persuaded to visit the college and be interviewed by the staff. He told them frankly how he felt.

"But Raju," they pressed him, "do you think that God has brought you where you are just so that you can make money?"

Because he is such a dear humble fellow, he was prepared to accept that they were in the right and he was in the wrong. So he allowed himself to be talked into the job. "I said, 'All right Lord, I'll do this work for three years, and I know you'll meet my needs.'" But as that time passed Raju knew that God was going to bless him with a well-paid job on his return to Hyderabad. And He would give Raju the desire of his heart in his own Christian literature work.

That's just what happened. Raju is now praying for an extra room in which people can come to look at his Christian books, and perhaps for personal counselling. "And if the room were big enough, or if there were a second room," he said with eyes shining, "we might have a Bible study and perhaps a Sunday School."

As we were eating our biryani, Raju and I discussed this problem of secular versus Christian employment. "It's a complex issue in India," he said. "There are parents to think about, brothers and sisters who need an education, and in-laws who must be provided for. When a believer works for a Christian group, the wage is often too low for their support."

"Of course God can supply those needs through other believers," I said.

"Yes, but sometimes God provides through secular jobs which pay a better wage. If a man has studied and earned qualifications, the secular job can support his family *and* Christian ventures."

I knew Raju himself supported four different pastors with his tithes so I could not argue with that. "It's so much easier in the West," I admitted. "A single believer is usually free to go off into full-time service without creating family hardships."

"But an Indian, whether he's married or not, has many people to consider," Raju said. "Normally he can't just say, 'God has told me to give up everything' and abandon his family and their needs."

I glanced at my watch and groaned. My appointment with Rev. Francis Sunderaraj was for 2.30 p.m. but it looked like I wouldn't make it. Raju and I rushed out to the busy street trying to flag down an autorickshaw, but they all whizzed by. A leper came up to me with stumps outstretched, pleading. This one touched my heart as few have done. I fumbled with some coins and reached out to him. Our eyes and hands met. But then 'untouchable' isn't one of God's words....

And still the autorickshaws ignored us. A spindly-legged fellow pedalled over to us in his battered cycle-rickshaw. It was something I'd always wanted to try. I wedged myself into the seat and we were off! Those spindly legs pedalled furiously on the level and then slowed down as we moved up a light slope. As the incline became steeper, our poor driver huffed and puffed, and finally got off and pushed us the rest of the way. It was good I wasn't catching a plane.

Francis Sunderaraj is the General Secretary of the Evangelical Fellowship of India, the association that unites India's evangelical Christian churches. EFI provides strength through fellowship and contacts, but it also has a valuable teaching arm, the CEEFI. Rev. Sunderaraj is a chemist by profession. As a young man he had a good salary from a firm who wished to give him further training. But with a clear call from God, against parental advice he left his job to prepare for the ministry.

"It was a big adjustment," he told me, laughing. "Going from a good salary to just eight rupees pocket money per month!" I couldn't resist grinning at Raju, recalling our earlier conversation. Apparently God had led these two men along very different paths!

"But the first year of seminary was very helpful," Rev. Sunderaraj continued. "The young people at Immanuel Church paid all my fees and supported me for the next two or three years. Gradually my pocket money increased to twenty rupees a month!"

As he described his theological training and early years in the ministry I recalled the words of St. Paul:

> It was He who gave some to be apostles, some to be prophets, some to be evangelists, and some to be pastors and teachers, to prepare God's people for works of service, so that the body of Christ may be built up.
>
> (Eph. 4:11,12)

Raju had certainly been directed to the secular career where God could best use him. On the other hand others, like

Francis Sunderaraj, were led out of secular work into Christian ministry. Clearly God desired to put his children in a wide range of positions and no one could say his was the only route for all to take. There was just one hard and fast rule for every Christian: *Follow God's personal directive to you.*

The conversation turned to the weaknesses and difficulties facing the Indian Church today. As I visited individual Christians throughout India, I saw men and women of great faith and sacrifice. Often it was difficult to find a single fault in these dear people! But surely faults there were. Sometimes these were more easily seen *en masse.* "What are the most pressing problems," I asked Rev. Sunderaraj, "currently in the national church?"

"Certainly the problems of nominalism," he said at once. "There are too many 'namesake' Christians who have never had a personal experience of Jesus. They may be numbered amongst the government statistics of 'Christians' in India, but are they listed in God's Book as members of the Body of Christ?

"We also suffer from lack of stewardship. Even many committed Christians are failing to give adequately to the work of Jesus Christ. Many pastors don't teach about tithing. This puts a strain on the health of the Church. It means we must depend on other sources for help.

"There's a lack of missionary awareness. In many places the church is thriving but it is only concerned about the immediate area. There are large parts of India where there is no Christian witness. The day of the Western missionary is past. It's up to Indian Christians to move into every state and be Christ's witnesses, some as teachers and pastors, and some in secular employment. It has been estimated that three to four thousand Indian missionaries are still needed to evangelise the millions of tribes here. Perhaps believers in the large Christian section of the North East should pray about 'going into Samaria' with the Gospel.

"Some churches suffer from false teaching," Rev. Sunderaraj went on. "On the one hand are those who preach the social gospel and on the other are the 'otherworldly' groups who are too introverted to exert a positive influence on their communities."

I asked Rev. Sunderaraj whether the caste system affected believers.

"Yes indeed," he said. "Caste differences should have no place in the Christian church, but they often do exist and create tensions. The caste system is basically evil. It's not like colour or tribal differences, it's a man-made system. 'We are all one in Christ Jesus,' the Bible tells us.

"God wants us to be good citizens of this country," he emphasized. "Our land has almost unbelievable problems. There will be a billion Indians by the end of the century. Slums, hardships and poverty will increase. We have ecological problems too. Our public places are filthy. God the Creator wants the environment to be healthy and clean, and Christians have a tremendous responsibility to set high standards in this area. We alone have a hope: for this life as well as the next. I believe that Christians working together must resolve to tackle these problems for the glory of the Lord Jesus Christ in India."

Sudershan and Raju, faithful younger brothers in the Lord, insisted on coming to the airport with me. Our car drove through the busy centre of the city at the evening rush hour. I looked out of the window to glimpse my last view of the Birla Temple, high above Hyderabad, local abode of Lord Venkataswara. Many pilgrims would be climbing the steep and narrow road to the marble temple now, supposing that it was he who guarded the city. I reflected on the numerous households throughout Hyderabad that I knew, in which families would be sitting together at their evening meal acknowledging that Jesus is Lord. They knew that it was the living Christ who looked down on Hyderabad, longing to pour out His blessing.

I saw again the texts so beautifully painted on the walls and thought once more of the unknown artist. I'd asked a number of people, but no one knew his name. They said he slips quietly into the city, does his work and moves on. I was sorry that I didn't get to know him, but perhaps he preferred to remain anonymous.

Raju, Sudershan and I waited in a travel office next to the air terminal, sharing private jokes to avoid sadder thoughts of parting. Then - to curious and uncomprehending glances - we bowed our heads and thanked God for this reunion. They each faced a period of uncertainty: Sudershan's hospital was about to close and he was looking for another job. Raju needed larger quarters to expand his literature work. But true to form they both showed more concern for me and my travels and work, as they prayed God's blessing on me.

I found my aisle seat, Row 21, on the flight to Delhi. The man in the window seat, I discovered as the plane soared heavenward, was a doctor working for UNESCO. He asked what brought me to India. When I mentioned my research into the spiritual experiences of Indian Christians, he was immediately intrigued. A Hindu, he expressed surprise that most of those I met had been born into Hindu homes, some from priestly families. I said that although backgrounds varied, they shared a desire to know the truth. I had noticed that the most common feature of their experiences was the prayer: "If there is a living God, reveal who You are to me!" Often they weren't looking for Jesus, but they found Him anyway.

"Do you believe in prayer?" I asked him.

"Yes, indeed," he said; "I have always said my prayers."

"And do you receive answers?" I asked.

He was quiet for a moment. "No," he admitted, "I have never had answers."

I recalled a TV interview with the late Shah of Persia: his final public appearance before he died. The interviewer asked him the same question. "I have never had answers," the Muslim monarch also replied.

"Man reaches out to God through a variety of religions," I said. "But if He doesn't respond, we need to think again." He thoughtfully agreed.

I said: "Don't you feel that God arranged our seating here? That He planned this conversation?"

"Oh yes," he said at once. "Actually, I had requested a

seat closer to the front. But they put me in Row 21. Obviously this was meant to be," he smiled.

"And I had planned to ask for a non-smoker," I said. "When I went to the desk I completely forgot to ask, and so was assigned this seat."

"I have no doubt He planned it, " he said again. We agreed to correspond and exchanged addresses, hoping to meet at some future date.

FIFTEEN

Choose life

The Lord is a refuge for the oppressed,
a stronghold in times of trouble.

Psalm 9:9

I was just settling into my large modern apartment near Lodi Gardens in Delhi when the bell rang. I opened the door to find a tiny lady with a smile that made up for her size.

"Miss Chandrabose?" I ventured. We embraced like old friends and scarcely stopped talking for four days....

Keya Chandrabose was brought up in a very beautiful home in East Bengal, set in almost twenty acres of land. A large temple was part of the spacious compound and in the courtyard there was enough space to seat over a thousand. She lived with her parents, brothers and sisters, uncles, aunts and cousins. There were sixty servants and live-in teachers. In Calcutta, too, there were other family houses.

The 1920's were a wonderful time to be growing up, with tables full of food, many friends coming and going in that vast house, and annual pilgrimages with all the family. But it was a strict household too. The children were expected to rise early, and to bathe in the family pond. Then they went to the temple in white clothes and offered food to the gods and goddesses. After that it was their duty to serve breakfast to their teachers.

In the evening the children gathered round and waited for a priest or elder cousin to come and tell stories. Some of these stories were beautiful, others were very exciting. But some were frightening. Often a priest would remind them: "If you don't obey the gods and goddesses they will come and break your bones."

Keya was particularly frightened of one god covered in snakes, and also the terrible goddess Kali. There were images everywhere in the large house, and their faces shocked her. She knew which rooms and which corners had the images she feared most, and she'd avert her eyes when she passed.

But soon it was 1930, and Keya was eight years old. It was the beginning of a new phase of her life. She was being prepared to go to Calcutta, to a 'mission' school. She didn't know what this was, but she expected she'd have to study hard. Keya knew about the Hindu goddess of knowledge, whom people prayed to for help with their studies. Her uncles and cousins had often advised: "Respect and fear these gods and goddesses. Then when you want something, they'll talk to you and help you."

It seemed a good idea to a young girl about to embark on a serious education. One morning she went down to the goddess's room. Keya closed the door and prostrated herself before the image. She shut her eyes tightly and waited to hear something wonderful, something that would let her know that her prayer was granted. When she finally looked up, her eyes fell on the arm of the image. A piece had been broken off and the shattered limb was exposed. It was only clay! Keya turned away from the room, bitterly disappointed.

A few days later it was time to say goodbye to her parents, her sisters and cousins, uncles, priests and teachers. Her grown-up brother took her to the Calcutta mission compound which was to play such a large part in her life and future.

Keya was very impressed by her teachers. They talked about a man named Jesus who used a tiny basket of food to feed five thousand people. Keya thought of her own parents, always kind to the poor and hungry. She thought of that vast courtyard where many great parties were held. But neither her father nor the priest would have been able to perform such a miracle for a hungry crowd. Keya thought of the many gods and goddesses at home. Of the many times she took food to them. *They* never gave food to *her*. She recalled the goddess with the broken arm, who did not respond to her prayer.

As the weeks went by Keya was introduced to many books

and a variety of subjects. And she heard more about Jesus to Whom the Christian teachers prayed, the One who fed the hungry and healed the sick.

Her brother finished Calcutta University and was now a school principal. He often came to visit her and she found, to her surprise and joy, that he knew about Jesus, having been invited to some Bible studies at the university. But later on she was puzzled when he said angrily: "Oh Christians. They're untouchable: they're such low caste, terrible people."

Keya looked at her Christian teachers even more carefully after that, and couldn't help loving them for their gentleness and kindness. Though they expected each child to work hard, they did not lose their tempers with them as her brother or older cousins often did.

"The more I heard about Jesus," Keya told me, "the more enthralled I became with this God of love. Here is a God," I reasoned, "one doesn't have to be afraid of!"

It came as a shock to young Keya the first time she saw two Christian classmates quarrel. "How can they be angry with each other?" she wondered. "Don't they know they worship a God of love? If I were a Christian," Keya mused, "I would be so happy I'd never quarrel."

"My favourite person was the school principal, Mrs. Grace," Keya told me. She was a missionary from the U.S.A. who had come to India with her family, but her children were killed in an accident shortly afterwards. She then searched for orphans in temples and hospitals, and wrote to officials offering to care for them. Before long she had eighty orphans whom she brought up as her 'children'. But many more passed through Grace Mission in the years to come. "The figures are the Lord's," she used to say, refusing to count heads and publicise numbers.

In those early days Keya observed Mrs. Grace's loving care for orphan children and developed a love for them herself. Once during a holiday visit to her brother's Calcutta home, Keya observed a five year old homeless boy, and her heart went out to him. She thought of Mrs. Grace. "Couldn't we put him in the hostel?" she pleaded.

Her brother's vehemence surprised her. "That *Christian* place? It's awful!" And that was the end of the subject.

Keya had learned to live with her brother's moods. On the one hand he had dutifully accepted full responsibility to look after her while she was at school in Calcutta. She accepted this transfer of authority so commonly practised within Indian families. It had seemed a practical solution for her parents, who lived a full two days journey from the boarding school. Her brother, resident in Calcutta, was the ideal choice of a substitute parent. But it was becoming increasingly clear to Keya that her brother did not approve of their choice of school and would have preferred to send her back to her parents.

Keya loved her life in the mission school, but when it was time to return home during the holidays, she looked forward to the two hundred mile journey home, by train, then steamer, then small boat up river to the village where her dear parents would be waiting. Then all the family - including twenty cousins - would go on a pilgrimage together.

Keya never forgot that summer she went home, secretly aware that she truly loved Jesus. She recalls how she was pampered and spoiled, how she climbed trees, and rode her favourite horse. She remembers praying silently to the Saviour and telling Him that she loved Him. It was to be her last carefree summer at home even though she was just ten years old.

Her brother had one love in his life, his beautiful four year old child. His other children had not lived so all his devotion was centred on this only son. Suddenly the child contracted a fever and two days later he died. Keya's brother went almost mad with grief.

He wrote a letter to Keya:

> I cannot deal with anything any longer. You'll have to return to our parents and study there. I think you should learn more about our religion and Bengali and other subjects. This is what you'll have to do.

> Then when you're twelve years old, you'll
> have to marry.

Keya could scarcely believe her eyes. "Leave this place?" she wondered desperately. "I'd be leaving my Jesus!" She hurried to the small prayer cell in the hostel, still holding the letter in her hand, and recalled the verse:

> Call upon Me in the day of trouble and I
> will deliver you.

Keya knelt down in the quiet room and prayed for a long time. Suddenly a senior girl opened the door and saw Keya there, with tears on her face. "Why are you crying?" she asked kindly. "If there's a problem why not go to Mrs. Grace? She is always willing to help."

Keya had never been to Mrs. Grace's private quarters before this. The older girl took her by the hand and they walked across the courtyard. Mrs. Grace came to the door and beckoned Keya inside. They sat together in Mrs. Grace's study and Keya showed the missionary her brother's letter. Mrs. Grace read it carefully and then looked at the girl: "What would you like to do?"

"I'd like to stay here."

"Then I'll do all I can to help you," the teacher said.

Mrs. Grace was so comforting, Keya felt she was like her own mother. But many problems remained. Would her family allow her to stay? How could she support herself? Keya went back to the hostel, and walked out onto the roof. The other children were in their rooms and everything was still. The sun was setting and it looked very beautiful but she was feeling miserable.

"I feel so lost and lonely," Keya prayed through her tears. "You come into my heart. Come and help me."

A gentle wind moved against her and a piece of paper fluttered at her feet. She stooped down to pick it up. It was a page from an old Bible and her eyes fell on the underscored verse:

> I have set before you life and death,
> blessings and curses. Now choose life so
> that you and your children may live, and
> that you may love the Lord your God,
> listen to His voice, and hold fast to Him.
> For the LORD is your life, and He will give
> you many years in the land.
>
> (Deut. 30:19-20)

The words thrilled Keya as nothing had ever done before. *Choose life!*

"Oh yes, I want life," she prayed eagerly, "I want Your life."

She held that paper in her hand, and at that moment she knew the Lord Jesus Himself was standing behind her, putting His hand on her head. What a glorious peace filled her! All fear was gone: the worry about her family...anxiety about her future...the fears of gods and goddesses...all disappeared.

When she wiped away her tears she found more verses underlined on the torn page:

> Be strong and courageous: do not be
> afraid or terrified because of them, for the
> Lord your God goes with you: He will
> never leave you nor forsake you.
>
> (Deut. 31:6)

With great joy in her heart, she left the roof and walked down the stairs. There was Mrs. Grace waiting for her. The missionary looked at Keya's radiant face and knew at once what had happened.

"The Lord is my Saviour now!" Keya exclaimed. "He is in my heart! He's with me," she added firmly, "and will not fail me!"

Keya's brother was in mourning, so he sent a friend to collect her. Bravely, Keya wrote a note and sent it with the friend:

I wish to remain here to study.

The following day she received a reply:

> You may stay on one condition. You must
> never tell our parents you are remaining in
> the hostel. You must never request funds if
> you want to stay. You are never to ask
> either our parents or me for finance. Give
> me your assurances in writing. If you don't,
> I shall have you taken from this place.

Keya found herself in a peculiar position. Although her brother despised the Christian school, it was clear that he no longer wished to be responsible for the care of his sister. Unbalanced by his bereavement, he was unwilling to communicate any of this to his parents. He just wanted to be left alone.

Keya accepted these immoderate demands quite simply because her discovery of Jesus Christ was now the paramount feature of her life. She read in the Bible about those who had "left all and followed Jesus." That she was but a child of eleven didn't matter. Her devotion had become as hardy as an adult's.

One point in her brother's letter seemed to comfirm her direction. She believed God had already told her: "Tell Me alone of your needs - not others." So Keya did not take offence at her brothers's harsh command. She looked on it as merely another reminder from God that she should depend on Him alone.

One day Keya was talking to Mrs. Grace about her plans. "If you give me the work to do," she said, "I know I'll be able to do anything!" Mrs. Grace took Keya's hand in hers:

"This is such a soft little hand! Will it be able to scrub this room?"

"Oh yes."

"Clean the floors?"

"Yes, Mrs. Grace."

"Sew, and keep house?"

"Yes, I'll be able!"

"Very well," Mrs. Grace smiled. "I shall pay you three annas for each curtain you sew; one anna for each duster...."

And all the tasks were listed with the small amounts Keya would receive for each. The girl readily agreed to everything; she knew God would not let her fail. Keya had come from a rich family and was never in want. As the youngest in the family she was the pampered darling of many. There was no need for her to learn to sew or mend or scrub or clean. All that was changed now. If she could stay, she knew she'd have to learn to earn her way.

So Keya's life changed dramatically. She began to rise before the others each morning, dust and clean and polish the stairs. She found a Naga girl named Lily who was expert at sewing and embroidery, and took lessons from her after school.

The principal was very particular, and often Keya would have to redo her work. I was puzzled about this. "Mrs. Grace was obviously very fond of you," I said to Keya. "Why did she make you work so hard? I should have thought she could have helped you financially."

"She did encourage me in many ways," Keya said, "and eventually helped me to get a scholarship to high school. But she was also aware that I wanted to earn my own way. I think she knew God was using these hardships to prepare me for the future."

That summer Keya's brother came to take her home for the holidays. The train ride, the steamer voyage, and finally the long journey up the river, were made in near silence. Her brother, still dark and sullen in his grief, alternately threatened Keya she'd not return to the mission and warned her not to tell.

Keya prayed earnestly that she could display the love of Jesus to her mother and her now ailing father. She longed to show them how happy she was, and also comfort them during her visit. On her arrival, Keya rushed into her father's room. He was in bed, nearly blind and paralysed by a stroke. He ran his hand over her face and wept. Keya's mother came in and the child's joy was complete. It seemed a lifetime since she had felt their arms around her.

That night as Keya prepared for bed her mother caressed her head gently and asked, "What is the change in you? Why do you seem so different?"

Keya was unable to keep her secret a moment longer. "I have found the true and living God," she whispered. Her mother put her hand to Keya's lips.

"Don't tell your brother," she advised.

It was a joy to Keya to be with her parents again but at the same time she often felt isolated and threatened. Her brother repeatedly told her she'd not return to Calcutta. Keya prayed: "Lord, soften his heart so that I can go back." She found it difficult to read her dear Bible and had to hide it behind another cover. She'd climb a tree with the 'book' and spend precious moments with God's Word.

Finally the holiday drew to a close. Reluctantly her brother said, "OK, let's go," and Keya knew her prayer had been answered. The journey back seemed never-ending. Finally the horse-carriage pulled up to the gate of the school. "Go ahead: go," her brother said coldly.

"What about my books - and my box - and my bedding?" Keya asked, not understanding.

"You want to stay there: then look after yourself," he said, and was gone.

Keya watched the carriage move away with her possessions in them Then she remembered her mother's last loving act: she had sewed a cloth pouch of five silver rupees into Keya's underclothes. Her Heavenly Father would meet every other need now.

Keya and I walked to an outdoor cafe in Lodi Gardens for our lunch. A picturesque thatched-roofed enclosure shaded us from the bright sunlight. She was enjoying every minute of her brief holiday. Her work involved long hours and she was now sixty-three, not as strong as she used to be. After lunch we sipped our drinks of *Thums Up* as I questioned her about those early days. "But did you have to go through such hardships?" I asked. "Couldn't you have written to your mother about this predicament?"

"I knew even from that age," Keya insisted, "that this was the way God wanted me to walk. Certainly there were problems and trials. But I praise God for those hard days now. I know how it feels to be poor."

Keya became proficient in all manner of housework and sewing, and was paid six rupees a month, which covered her hostel and school fees. She found joy in doing even the smallest tasks for the Lord Jesus.

"He was so close, you see," explained Keya. "I never lost the sense of His presence. Of course I worked hard, but I was never unhappy."

Keya's father passed away when she was thirteen. She returned home to spend the month in traditional Hindu mourning. It was a difficult time for the young teenager. She was anxious to show respect to the family and to comfort her mother, but she found it hard to live through rituals in which she no longer believed.

"The Lord Jesus was simply the most important person in my life," Keya said as we walked through the gardens. "Nothing mattered: no discomfort, no misunderstandings. He alone was everything I could want or need."

"Do you think your mother understood your new faith?" I asked her. "Did she realise what you were going through?"

"She knew I loved Jesus, but wanted me to say as little as possible, even to her. Humanly speaking my life was in the hands of my brother now, and elder male relatives. Even if she had known of my hardships, to expose them would have made things worse. But I never doubted her love for me."

Keya returned to Calcutta and won a scholarship to High School. Then she went down with malaria, dysentery and other infections, and lost a year of schooling.

There were times when Hindu classmates laughed at the serious young Christian who often spoke about Jesus to them. Even girls who claimed to be Christians teased her, saying she was 'too religious'. One Hindu friend observed: "What does your God do for you, anyway? Look at all your hardships! You get abuse, you're constantly working, you don't get enough books, you don't even get proper nourishment. A fine job He's doing taking care of you!"

Keya thought of the Apostle Paul and how he had to make tents for a living. That inspired her! She also recalled how Jesus left the wealth of heaven and became poor for our sakes: it was a voluntary sacrifice 'to bring many sons to glory'.

One day some Christian friends asked Keya to form a prayer group. That same year, she went to the missionary and announced: "Mrs. Grace, I must be baptised!"

The principal, now approaching retirement, knew this would cause great suffering to her young friend. Dr. and Mrs. Hopkins, about to become the next superintendents of the mission, questioned Keya carefully.

"I love Jesus," Keya told them. "I have loved Him all these years. I cannot hide it any longer."

Her High School principal asked her: "Have you thought of the consequences?"

Keya replied: "I thought of them a long time ago..."

One day her brother arrived to settle the matter. "If you do this," he warned, "you'll be deprived of property and disowned by your family."

"I accept that," Keya said quietly.

"I want you to put in writing that you'll never ask for any property or money from us."

Keya sat down at once and wrote out the letter.

Her brother-in-law, a kindly man, also came to see her. "You know you're still young," he said gently. "If you think this is the truth for you, then I have nothing to say. But think of the others! Think of your mother: she'll die!"

"I am praying that the Lord will strengthen her heart," Keya said.

November 3 1940. Keya was sixteen years old. Her Hindu classmates and teachers joined her Christian friends and they all went to her church to witness her baptism. Keya's brother-in-law returned. "Is it done?"

"It is done," said Keya. "Of course."

"Does your brother know?"

"I've written a letter renouncing any claims, as he suggested."

The brother-in-law shook his head sadly.

Keya's brother returned. "Is it done?"

"Yes."

"Shame, shame, shame!" he cried. "Such a shame to the family!"

Keya was told she couldn't go home anymore. Her mother became ill at the news. At the end of that school year, Keya's kindly brother-in-law came secretly to give her a warning.

"Some of your elder relatives are planning to take you by force to the Kali temple."

Keya knew what that meant: they would shave her head and pour cow dung on it. "How soon?" she asked, but he could not say.

Mrs. Grace asked, "What was the verse God gave you that first day?"

Keya quoted:

> Be strong and courageous. Do not be afraid or terrified because of them, for the Lord your God goes with you: He will never leave you nor forsake you.

"Do you still believe it?" asked Mrs. Grace.

"Oh yes," exclaimed Keya. "Even more now, after all these years."

A missionary friend in another district needed help and was happy to take Keya, who welcomed the prospect of working with children. She was there only a few weeks when word came that her brother was searching mission schools in the area. She was sent to a new station, alone, on the train.

"In those days," Keya told me, "no young girl ever travelled alone. Several times I was in danger, but I knew God was with me."

Over the next few years Keya was threatened many times by her relatives and came close to being taken off by force. That could have meant confinement in a house or a forced marriage. She became proficient at the art of hasty departures, once making her getaway on the back of a truck behind the oil tins.

She remembers one journey that included a ride through the jungle on the back of a buffalo cart. The sun was setting when they started out. The evening was beautiful as the oxen lumbered along, while the two drivers sat up front murmuring to each other. The darkness drew over them quickly, and the stars shone with a richness she had never seen before. Keya started to sing:

I've started my journey
But on my journey
There will be storms
And all kinds of difficulties.
But I'm not afraid
Because You are the Pilot of my life.
I'm not afraid.

SIXTEEN

The beautiful home

The morning will surely come,
the darkness will vanish
and thy voice pour down in golden streams
breaking through the sky.

Rabrindrath Tagore
Gitanjali

It was time for Keya to make a decision. What would she do in the future? She had the opportunity to attend a well-known Ladies' College, but she wasn't sure what to do. She'd heard that it was a rich society girl's college, and Mrs. Grace feared she'd be wrongly influenced.

Keya was determined to fast and pray until she received an answer. Several days later she rushed to Mrs. Grace with the joyous news. God had called her *by name* and told her she should go!

Mrs. Grace had always trusted her young companion but hoped in this case she wasn't mistaken. The old missionary wept as Keya packed her small bag and prepared to leave.

The Ladies' College stood on thirty acres of land with a swimming pool, sports courts, fruit trees and rose gardens. The buildings were beautiful, and when Keya was shown to her room she almost gasped at the marvellous bathroom, hot water and western-style toilet. It was luxury indeed..

Her guide returned to take her to lunch. "Do you have a lot of money with you?" she asked.

"Yes," said Keya. "I have five rupees!"

The girl looked at her strangely. "That's alright. You needn't tell anyone."

As they approached the dining room she thought of mealtimes back home, with the family sitting on mats on the floor. The brass plates were spread on a low table and to her young eyes it had always looked very grand. The college dining room was another revelation. It was laid out in western style, with Burma Teak tables, tablecloths and cutlery. Keya didn't know how to use a knife and fork, and for days she could hardly eat anything!

Keya's clothes set her apart from the other girls from the start. She wore coarse white sarees, and was only too well aware of the other students' gaily coloured silks and organdies.

On the second evening she walked to the deserted tennis court in the moonlight and sat on a bench. "Lord," she prayed, "I don't feel I belong in this place. Was that call real? I thought I heard Your voice, but You'll have to show me again!"

In a moment a young South Indian woman came and sat beside her. They began talking and Keya learnt that she was from the Mar Thoma Church. Keya sensed genuine friendship at once, and grasped the young woman's hand in her enthusiasm. The next day she was horrified to learn that she'd held the hand of the Vice-Principal!

It was a droll start to her academic career but she soon settled in to the routine and became an accepted and respected member of the student faculty. In time she started prayer cells that operated throughout the college.

In six long years, Keya did not see her mother. Then word came that she was ill, and her brother-in-law agreed to accompany her back home. It was a thrill for her to retrace her steps back in time, first on the familiar train, then the steamer, then the small boat up the river. But her mother's appearance gave her a shock.

She looked an old woman now, scarcely more than skin and bones. "Dear God," Keya wept, "have I done this to her?" But at the same time, she knew her mother was in God's hands.

If Keya hoped there would be a welcoming atmosphere on arrival, her cousins provided a hasty answer. She was not allowed to go to her old room or even to her mother's. Instead a cot was made up on the covered verandah.

On the third morning a cousin, the acting head of the family, called Keya to his house. They stood in the courtyard as he offered her a brass bowl of milk. His little three year old clamoured to drink some from it, but the cousin hastily forbad it. Keya hadn't realised her mother was standing in the doorway watching.

The cousin said: "Drink it," and Keya lifted the bowl to her lips, feeling uneasy without knowing why. Just then her mother came forward and snatched the bowl from her hands, flinging the contents into a nearby ditch. An hour later a cat was found dead on that very spot.

"Take her to Calcutta in the morning," her mother ordered her brother-in-law. "She is not safe here." Hastily she prepared Keya's favourite foods and wrapped them with her clothes.

Keya clung to her mother's feet as they said farewell the next morning. "I fear no more about you!" the older woman said with love and pride as they embraced. Keya knew now that her mother accepted her just as she was.

In her last year of college, Keya became very ill. The diagnosis was malignant malaria and for almost two months she was very near death. The doctor said that if she did survive she would probably be of no use to anyone as brain damage would result in severe memory loss.

All were amazed, therefore, when she returned to college to sit her exams. Everyone had considered this impossible. She was still very thin and weak, and had lost almost all of her beautiful thick hair. But she took her psychology exams and got very high grades!

All these years Grace Mission was home to Keya. After graduation she became a hostel superintendent there, and in time was appointed headmistress of the school she had entered as an eight year old girl.

Then Keya received a telegram saying that her mother was very ill. Her brother-in-law took matters into his own hands and removed the dying woman to his Calcutta home. Keya went there every day after work and stayed with her until the following morning. They were precious months for the two women, with Keya now able to care for her mother and also speak freely about her faith. When visitors came to see the sick woman, she told them proudly: "This is my best child!"

Towards the end, Keya contacted her brother. He and his wife, embittered for so many years, agreed to visit her home at the Mission - and even to stay.

One day as Keya sat alone with her mother, she said: "I want to see you in heaven." The woman, too weak to talk, shed a few tears and smiled, putting her hand on her daughter's head. It was then that Keya felt her mother had opened her heart to Jesus.

The following day, April 14, 1951, Keya's brother and sister-in-law stood on one side of the bed, and Keya on the other. Her mother raised herself slightly and put her hands on the head of the husband and wife.

"Forgive everyone," she whispered. "Love everyone."

Then she turned to Keya. "Forget all bitterness," she whispered, holding her hand. "Love them."

She sank back, and lay still.

"*Ma Keya*," she called suddenly.

"Yes?"

"I'm going home."

"Which home?"

"Can't you see the beautiful home?" ....and she breathed her last.

SEVENTEEN

The principal

> *You are the light of the world....*
> *let your light shine before men,*
> *that they may see your good deeds*
> *and praise your Father in heaven.*
>
> **Matt. 5:14,16**

Keya's scholarship for post-graduate study in the U.S. came as a complete surprise. She hadn't even applied for it! Before she knew what was happening, in 1952 she was on her way to Northwestern University to study religious and elementary education.

It wasn't just the splendid campus and equipment, the friendly people and the new sights. What amazed her most of all was the generosity of Christian people. Wherever she went, she was asked to speak. It was an honour to be asked, she felt. But afterwards, they'd press a cheque into her hand. She'd try to decline. "Give it to missions," she'd plead. They just laughed.

It did give her some wonderful opportunities to send money home, to provide more milk for the children or some equipment for the hostel. Keya did well in her course, and obtained her M.A.

On returning to India, Keya spent four years as a district evangelist for her church. She was then called to a Regional High School in West Bengal as principal and headmistress, and this became her life's work.

The school had been built for famine children eighty-five years earlier, and more recently the military had taken over the buildings. By the time Keya arrived in 1958, the buildings had been declared unsafe and classes had to be held under the trees. This presented new problems: goats and cows would eat up the girls' books and clothes!

There had been one hundred and fifty girls at the school when Keya took over. Within her first three months there were three hundred students, and the school boasted telephones, lights, electricity and official recognition! There are now nine hundred in the high school and six hundred in other departments.

Over the years the work has advanced on four fronts: children, staff, buildings and funds. Keya couldn't ignore the needy children around her - like the thirty-nine starving orphans she found in the first few years, the babies she tended in her rooms, or the boys she raised as her own. But that meant that both the hostel and the school needed more staff and new buildings. These included a beautiful new chapel and more recently a dining hall.

Teachers' salaries were paid by the government, Keya's was paid by the Mission, and church groups gave financial support. But more funds were needed. For this reason over the years Keya began various income-generating projects. She started a poultry unit with purchases of layers, broilers and cockerels. She realised twelve thousand Rs. from cows' milk and ten thousand Rs. from a fishery in one year. Less profit came from the vegetable and fruit gardens. Keya also encouraged various craft projects such as basket-making to work towards becoming self-supporting.

Keya's days as a district evangelist prepared her to develop other ministries. A Rural Women's Development Project covered other parts of West Bengal and Bihar. There were district evangelists, supervisors of village schools, and child care, adult literacy and self-help projects.

Keya was no stranger to confrontation, and she now faced legal and civic battles as the work of the school expanded. The first crisis came in her first month because she decided to fence in the school area to keep out animals and wandering villagers when school was in session. Although the property belonged to the school, a band of angry locals got so carried away with their protests that they threatened to kill her. Finally the police restored order.

During the 1960 drought, the water crisis caused anxiety everywhere. The school's water bills rose sharply. Since coal mines had been worked underneath the property, the colliery proprietor came to Keya's assistance. He pulled out the underground map of the area and found the spot most likely to produce water. Unfortunately it was not only the wells that were running dry. Keya's funds were fast running out due to the exploration work. The engineers arrived and began to bore down in the predicted place. They kept digging but they found nothing.

It was a time of great stress and Keya went off to a cooler place for a brief rest. One day during a period of prayer and fasting, she had a vision of Jesus. He was saying that fifty feet down on the north east corner of the property there would be much water. Three times He said this! Keya got off her knees and wrote immediately to the school.

When she returned she was thrilled to see a well dug on the spot of her vision. There was so much water they had to employ three shifts of people to get it up! "There have been many droughts since then," Keya laughed, "but *this* well has never dried up!"

More recently a false accusation was made against Keya and the antagonist took her to court. The case was to be heard on a Monday, and Keya spent the weekend in prayer and fasting. On Monday morning Keya's accuser was coming out of his house when he was struck down with a terrible stomach ache. He had to be carried in again! The case was heard anyway, and decided in Keya's favour. A Hindu lawyer came over to her afterwards and looked at her suspiciously. "I studied in a missionary college," he said. "I have seen missionaries on their knees when they are in trouble. Their prayers were answered." He wagged his finger at Keya. "You must have done that, too!"

Her wonderful melodious laugh rang down the hall.

I read in the *HINDU* today one reader's view that people are only converted to Christianity 'through bribery or brainwashing'. The letter went on to say that efforts made to proselytise would be put to better use in raising the living standards of the people.....

Over the years Keya took care of many children who in time became science, commerce or arts graduates. Although most of them made a commitment to the Christian faith in the early days, some drifted away from those beliefs in later years. "It was very sad," Keya said, "but one could do no more than wait for the time they wanted to return. That is what is so unique about the Christian faith. It cannot be forced on anyone. You cannot be brain-washed or bribed into accepting Jesus! It is only through the gentle wooing of the Holy Spirit that anyone can come to Christ. It is a totally personal thing between God and the individual. Anything other than that is not Christ's teaching.

"That's why Hindu children are not 'at risk' in Christian institutions," she went on. "We cannot 'convert' them. We just live the Christian life where we are. But we cannot pressurize anyone into accepting Christ!"

"The Christian can change the world in two ways," Keya told me the next day. "He must live a life that reflects Jesus Christ: *and he can pray!*"

I thought of something Mahatma Ghandi said a long time ago:

> If every Christian in India lived according
> to the teachings of Jesus Christ there
> wouldn't be a Hindu left in India.

EIGHTEEN

A Sikh finds

We should worship the Name,
believe in the Name
which is ever and ever the same.
Meditate on the grace of the true Name.....
for emancipation is by grace alone.....

Guru Nanak
Japji

One afternoon Keya agreed to join me on some visits. Our taxi drove us past many rows of splendid white houses on Greater Kailash and finally to the one marked *Y.L. Malik.* A distinguished looking gentleman greeted us at the door and ushered us inside. We were introduced to his wife and sat down surrounded by beautiful things, but they were outshone by the fellowship shared by four strangers that early evening in November. Keya and I listened with fascination to this handsome couple, once Hindu disciples of the Dayal Bagh gurus in Agra who had discovered, ten years earlier, that Jesus Christ was the only means of salvation. "He has brought us peace," Mr Malik said simply.

I reflected on the varied backgrounds into which we four were born. Though coming disparate ways, though strangers only minutes earlier, we savoured a oneness impossible outside of Christ. But God had another surprise in store.

As we talked together, a motorcycle roared up outside, and soon a young man entered the room. Mr. Malik introduced him as Sukhwant Singh. Born in Darjeeling in 1961, Sukhwant was taught as a child from the *Granth Sahib*, the book of the Sikhs. He learnt about the eleventh guru who would lead him to God, and was very conscious of Him from an early age. "I pictured Him as a Superman who could do everything," he recalls, "and I would often pray and tell Him what I needed. My concept of God was not tied to any human form or name."

But Sukhwant also enjoyed mischief. He lied and cheated, made fools of his teachers and stole from shops. If he thought about his sin it was only to tell himself that there were many people a good deal worse. His father conscientiously instructed him in the proper standards to follow. He taught him to use will-power to live a successful life and stressed the importance of achievement.

At college in Batala, Sukhwant began to think more seriously, beginning to wonder: "Is there anyone listening to me? Are my prayers heard? If God is there, what is His Name?" Conscious of his father's teaching he began to establish rules for his own conduct. He set certain standards to conform to the image he had of himself. It disturbed him, however, to find that he could not always keep his own rules. He had to acknowledge his failings.

"It is said that Sikhs are truly seekers," Sukhwant explained to me. "They spend their life seeking for meaning, and when they find it they no longer belong on earth. It is then that they're taken to heaven, to a new and blissful state."

True to this spirit Sukhwant asked his friends about their beliefs but no one was able to give him satisfactory answers. In his second year he drifted into a depression. He knew he could do well but he could see no purpose in life, and was distressed at his failure to find answers to his questions. "I concluded that no God does exist," he said, "but saying that brought even less peace to my heart." His teachers and parents were disappointed with his performance and restlessness. "Why don't you study and do well?" they pressed him.

There was one thing that kept Sukhwant's life together: pride. He was too proud to lower himself to take drugs, and felt contemptuous of anyone who did. And he resolved to keep himself from any immoral associations, and remain pure until marriage. He was a keen sportsman, and was successful in basketball, the high jump, pole-vaulting and the one hundred and two hundred metres. He won meets at the state level in 1979.

But as depression grew it ruined his sporting activity. He

found himself becoming short-tempered and angry. He learned karate but began to misuse it, fighting frequently with people and hurting them. His parents were beside themselves as they saw deterioration in their eldest child. He would strike his sisters and brother in a rage, and even tried to strike his father. His mother cried: "It would have been better if you had not been born!"

At this unhappy stage in his life, he became friendly with a nominal Christian girl. She was a free-living girl whose standards were not like his own, and soon Sukhwant concluded, "All Christian girls must be like this." Then he broke his own moral code that had at one time meant so much to him, and could not forgive himself. He felt a duty to marry her, but she simply laughed and did not take him seriously. He said to himself: "How could there be a God who failed to protect me from this evil?" But at the same time, he could not *blame* God, since He did not exist! Sukhwant knew that he had only himself to blame, but this made it harder still.

In the beginning of his third year, he met a Christian student by the name of Arup Das. Sometimes students laughingly nicknamed him the 'Holy Man'. Sukhwant could see that he was good at sport and at his studies, and that he set a true Christian example. One day Arup spoke to Sukhwant about Jesus Christ. Sukhwant suddenly realised that of all the students he had asked about their religious views, he had never approached this fellow. And so now he did so. Sukhwant was impressed that Arup did not need to stop to think, or scratch his head, like the others. He spoke with conviction, and answered each question from the Bible. Arup opened his Book and pointed to a passage, and asked Sukhwant to read it! There was no hesitation here! The fellow knew what he believed all right.

"For the first time," said Sukhwant, "I heard the claims of the Bible and I was amazed. I longed to know more. And what impressed me most was the fact that *God can and will forgive and forget.*"

But his Christian friend told him: "In order to receive forgiveness, you must commit your life to Jesus Christ. He

must become your Lord and Saviour." Sukhwant baulked at
this. After all, there was such a wide world out there, and so
many different beliefs! It seemed to him too narrow a way.
"Only Jesus?" Well, he admitted, when his friend spoke it
did seem just what he needed. Sukhwant was driven back to
other scriptures. He searched his own holy books, the *Gita*,
the *Koran*, and parts of *Ramayana*. It became his greatest
study, so that he neglected the rest of his work, barely
passing his other subjects. It seemed to him this was the
most pressing and urgent project!

But the more he read, the more he was convinced that
the Bible and Jesus Christ stood alone. Nothing compared
with the Christian way. At the end of his third year, he had
discovered that nine key verses gave him a perfect guide-line
for his life. Whatever questions he had were answered in
these verses, which spoke of sin and forgiveness, of Christ
and the new birth. It only remained for him to obey or
reject them. "And since I had already asked God to show me
the way," Sukhwant said, "it would have been foolish to
reject what He was showing me."

Only the last verse disturbed him somewhat, as if there
were still something incomplete about these steps:

> "Here I am! I stand at the door and knock.
> If anyone hears my voice and opens the
> door, I will come in and eat with him and
> he with Me."
>
> (Rev. 3:20)

Then Sukhwant discovered the key that unlocked everything
to him. It was found in John's Gospel.

> Until now you have not asked for anything
> in My name. Ask and you will receive, and
> your joy will be complete.
>
> (John 16:24)

The light burst into his life. "I did not ask," he wanted to
shout. "I asked gurus, I asked Sai Baba, I asked students and

read many scriptures. But I did not ask Jesus! What am I waiting for?" It was 3 p.m. on July 25, 1981 when Sukhwant asked. He asked Jesus to forgive his sins and at once he had the assurance that this was done. He asked for a personal relationship with God, and received it! And he prayed for help to share with others what he himself had found. Arup was overjoyed and the two boys began Bible studies together. But when he told his 'Christian' girlfriend, he met with only scorn for his decision. Realising her allegiance was false he broke off the relationship.

Sukhwant wondered how he could show his friends and family how much Jesus meant to him. Reading his Bible one morning he came upon these words:

> If a man has long hair it is a disgrace to
> him.
>
> (1 Corinthians 11:14)

He did not want to do anything disgraceful for a follower of Jesus Christ so he removed his turban and cut his hair, praying for strength not to let his Saviour down.

His decision to become a Christian had caused little disturbance among his friends and family. They were pleased with his efforts to 'turn over a new leaf', although they showed little understanding of his spiritual discovery. He could 'go that way to God' if he wished. But cutting his hair was different.

"You have fallen from your caste," his mother shouted angrily. His father ordered him out of the house and stopped providing any money for Sukhwant's education or clothes. Sukhwant had to find jobs to support himself and meet his college needs. But he was determined to prove the faithfulness of the Lord Jesus and the change in his life.

When he was thrown out of his home, Sukhwant went to stay with Arup. He wondered whether to give up his studies, but felt that God wanted him to return home, and began to pray about this. On the tenth day, his mother came to see him. Weeping, she asked him to come back, wanting Sukhwant to forgive *her* for behaving badly. He returned to his family, though his angry father refused to support him. "If you say that Jesus is everything," he told his son, "let Him provide for your schooling and clothes and expenses."

Sukhwant found many small jobs, paid his way through college and was the first from his class to obtain a job! He worked hard and gradually increased his earnings, putting aside ten percent for God's work and saving as much as he could. When his father had business difficulties, Sukhwant wrote out a large cheque and sent it to him as a gift. "I want you to know that Jesus has kept me this way," he said.

Later Sukhwant joined the Delhi Bible Fellowship pastoral team as a full-time assistant pastor. "My parents have finally seen a real change in my life," he told me, "and my younger sisters are now believers," he added, his face breaking into a big smile as he looked at Keya and myself.

Before we parted, Sukhwant prayed for us: for Keya, returning on the morrow to her post in West Bengal; for the Maliks and their children; for me. I stole a glance at him as he prayed. And some say there's no such thing as a miracle!

NINETEEN

A man named Luke

They come with their laws and their codes
to bind me fast
but I evade them for ever,
for I am only waiting for love
to give myself up at last into His hands.

Rabrindrath Tagore
Gitanjali

The studious-looking, quietly-spoken young man with a wispy beard didn't exactly fit my picture of a drug-taking tearaway. But then I wasn't looking at the old Luke Samson. Luke is today working full-time in slum redevelopment in Delhi but there was a time when his own life needed redeveloping....

Luke's father was an Indian Jew who had converted to Catholicism when he married Luke's mother, a Goan Catholic. He was a doctor and head of a pharmaceutical company in Bombay. That's where Luke and his six brothers and sisters grew up. It was a well-to-do family and the children were all spoilt but well-loved by their parents. Dr. Samson was not only managing director of the Indian company but a director of firms in Britain and the States. Despite a very full professional career, he made his family his top priority. He taught them firm principles, but it was his love that was the best teacher. Luke admired his father. He too was determined to make it to the top and own a Mercedes or Jaguar. His father indulged him as much as he could.

"We were all shattered when he died suddenly of a heart attack in 1971," Luke told me. It triggered off the slow disintegration of a once-prosperous, close and loving family. Luke's mother was devastated and for a time was unable to cope with the necessary affairs of the home and business. Soon those she trusted cheated her of money and the family incurred great financial loss.

Luke felt let down by God and began to question the Catholic rituals which were bringing him no meaning or peace. "All I had was a big emotional void," he says of that time.

He became bitter towards family and friends who seemed indifferent to his loss. When his closest brother left for the U.S.A. to study, he felt he had lost everything. There now seemed to be no purpose in studying or working . He had entered a good college but he dropped out after one year. He began to use hashish, then LSD, and took 'uppers' and 'downers' as well. When he first blacked out, it didn't bother him. His thoughts were often on death, anyway.

"He's on drugs, Mother," his sister announced at the breakfast table one day. Luke's mother tried a loving and compassionate approach, and begged Luke to be open with her. Despite his love for his mother and his guilt at hurting her, he embarked on a course to destroy himself and bring her even more grief. He drifted into more frequent use of drugs and began to spend huge sums of money on them. It was inevitable that he'd turn to stealing to support his habit, and he forged cheques using his mother's signature. A black depression crept over him. In seeking to escape it he used drugs and money to achieve a very temporary euphoria. Money slipped through his fingers as the cost of his drug-consumption rose. He flitted in and out of five-star hotels, running up bills. He was only nineteen years old.

Luke's portion from his father's estate was soon whittled away. Mounting debts at home meant that Mrs. Samson was obliged to sell furniture and antiques to support the family. She found a job but by this time four more of the children were on drugs and drained her of her resources. "At this time I went away for long periods," Luke explained to me, "conning people to get more money. I knew funds were low at home so I went elsewhere and was prepared to tell any stories to get whatever I could. I lived on the streets or with friends; I was jailed several times. I tried my hand at making money but I wasn't successful." This was the young man who only a few years earlier had had visions of 'the best of everything', when he imagined that the world was at his feet.

As Luke was overdosing on LSD, his mother had a nervous breakdown. She couldn't cope with the disintegration of the family and was hospitalised in 1976. Luke, too, wound up in hospital through drug abuse. But when released, he continued to make deals to support his habit. Even money intended for his younger brothers' and sisters' school fees went on drugs.

In 1977 he left home again, lived on the street for a time, and then joined up with a rock band, carrying their equipment. After a time with them he drifted away, and went into the mountains where he studied and practised *rajayoga*, 'the meditation of kings', in which the student tries to come to a state of mental calm through breathing exercises. During this period Luke was forced to sit and think about himself and his life. He came face to face with his weaknesses, past errors, and unhelpful attitudes and values. He tried to look at himself objectively, imagining that he was God. It helped him to feel removed from his own shortcomings, but also reinforced a suspicion that God might exist after all. And it created within him a longing to relate to someone far greater than himself. In the mountains and living with the *sadhus*, he came to see the hypocrisy and emptiness of their lives. The truth must be somewhere else.

"I found that even at this time I could not erase the attachment to Christ I had had since childhood," Luke told me. "Now I found myself trying to answer the question, 'Are you still denying Me, Luke?' - an inner impression which I kept trying to ignore." But his mind distorted by drugs, Luke was unable to think clearly.

Whilst in the mountains he began to deal in drugs. He found out where the best hashish in the world was available, and soon established himself as part of a chain of dealers. This was dangerous territory, however, and Luke was treated treacherously when he tried to help a fellow junkie. Disillusioned and sceptical, he drifted down to Delhi with *charas* (purified hashish) to sell at the university. He reached another dead-end, broke, as 1978 was drawing to a close.

A drug-taking friend told Luke about a Christian community called *Ashiana*, which offered help to addicts, and Luke decided to see what was on offer. The community was quite new, and its members were not very experienced. Other addicts were able to slip Luke drugs when he needed them, and the experiment did not help him. When the Christians tried to explain a better way, Luke's preoccupation with himself and his feelings stopped him seeing any other point of view.

By now he was alternating between hallucinations and depression. The euphoria had gone and despair was never far away. A wrist injury made him feel worse but it served one good purpose. He'd been asked to do a *scam*, a drug run out of the country, and now that was given to someone else. A narrow escape, he was to feel later on.

Luke had been on drugs eight years now, and he was just twenty-three years old. He was totally enslaved, yet each fix gave him nothing but the blues. The Samsons' house in Bombay had to be sold and the family moved to Pune. Luke drifted from Bombay to Pune to Goa, and finally decided to return to Ashiana in Delhi.

"They were willing to take me in again," Luke said. "And this time I began to listen to what they said. I became more God-conscious, and at the same time more aware of myself as a totally fallible human being. In the evenings the members did studies in the Epistles of John and James and although I didn't have to attend, I started to go. One night they read the passage,

> Anyone who claims to be in the light but hates his brother is still in the darkness. Whoever loves his brother lives in the light, and there is nothing in him to make him stumble. But whoever hates his brother is in darkness and walks around in the darkness; he does not know where he is going, because the darkness has blinded him.

> (1 John 2:9-11)

"I thought of my own hatred: resentment of authority, of the police, of the establishment. I had feelings of hatred towards friends who tried to help, even towards several in Ashiana whom I mistrusted. I felt very challenged by who God really was and who I was in relation to Him. I was now ready to accept that I didn't know who God was. That was when I very sincerely asked: 'God, if you really exist, reveal Yourself to me'."

All this was in June 1979. And now Luke began to feel deep down that God was responding. He found himself daily uttering cries for help, asking God to take the depression from him. And he sensed that depression lifting! He began to feel the strength to make the right decisions where once he didn't have that freedom.

Luke's drug habit was still there, but it had decreased. For a long time he had been 'stoned' virtually all day long, and from morning to night he'd take anything he could lay his hands on. He'd still take drugs several times a day, but this was a great improvement!

Three days after uttering that 'if-you-exist' prayer Luke went to his room and locked the door. He got down on his knees and began to pray.

"God, I really want to lead the right kind of life and choose the right path. I want to turn away from what I've been doing and not live that kind of life any longer. I want to follow You, Jesus."

Within the hour a deep healing flooded him for the loss of his father and the insecurity that had plagued him all those years. This healing came in the awareness of his Heavenly Father's love and all the security that brings. "But more important, that wave of new life brought *forgiveness*," Luke said. "I'd been through 'good boy/bad boy' cycles before, but I knew this wasn't that. There was a cleansing I never knew until now. I was totally identified with Christ."

Luke's existence had been built around drugs for more than eight years, when he had spent times in an almost permanent state of hallucination. Doctors had diagnosed brain damage, but in the months to come all such effects were worked out of his blood and brain and he became physically, as well as spiritually, a whole man.

That September he began a new job doing social work in a slum. For the first time he 'came clean' with a prospective employer and told him the hard facts of his life. And the man still took him on. Luke continued to live in the Ashiana house, and joined in the Bible studies eagerly. He became a worker there, beginning to help others who drifted in to the community. At the end of the year he realised he was being directed to do slum redevelopment work full-time.

After Luke committed his life to Christ his two sisters and their husbands followed him in that step, and also joined the Ashiana Community. One couple work in the drug-rehabilitation side of the work, and the others are involved with slum redevelopment. His brother, also an ex-addict, is now working in drug rehabilitation.

"The family has come together again," Luke was happy to report, "now that our lives are based on Christ. Mother always had a deep relationship with Jesus; she used to spend continuous hours in prayer. Now she's very happy again after all those painful years. There's also a new generation - her grandchildren - which reminds us all of the new start God has given us."

TWENTY

Reconciliation

*But now in Christ Jesus you who
once were far away have been brought
near through the blood of Christ.
For He Himself is our peace, Who has
made the two one and has destroyed
the barrier, the dividing wall of
hostility.*

Eph. 2:13-14

I arrived in Pune early in the evening, to a pink sky and long
shadows across the tarmac. The tiny airport is a perfect size:
a few dozen steps from airfield to waiting car.

My borrowed apartment looked wonderful as usual, and
Anthony, faithful manager and cook, was waiting at the
door. Anthony is a Catholic with a real enthusiasm for the
Lord Jesus. On a previous trip he had insisted on preparing
my rooms and meals despite a slipped disc that caused him
agony. Using his bike was too painful, so he had to walk to
the shops and flats he tended.

That was the year I learnt that a group of Catholic
brothers had formed a Full Gospel Businessmen's chapter in
Pune. They came to the flat for a meeting, and their living
faith was a great encouragement. One by one they shared
accounts of the crisis experiences that brought them to a
personal relationship with Jesus Christ.

Anthony came in then with a large tray, and served coffee
and biscuits. He was obviously still in pain, and I told the
others about it. Someone said: "Anthony! Sit down on this
chair!" Anthony obeyed, but didn't understand. One of the
men explained: "We're going to ask Jesus to heal you. Do
you believe He can do so?"

"Yes I do," Anthony replied, but it was clear that his own
prayers were of the more traditional and respectable kind.
He looked apprehensive as the cluster of men came towards

him on all sides and laid hands on his head.

Anthony never figured out how it happened but within a moment of the last "Amen" he was bounding out of the chair with a new sound on his lips. "Jesus healed me! Jesus healed me!" he exclaimed as he began to twist and turn, his arms upward.

He said later: "I always thought that pain was a gift from Jesus. We could enter His suffering that way, and bear a cross with Him."

I said: "But we're told that the prayer of faith will make the sick person well (James 5). Jesus healed everyone who asked Him when He lived on earth. I believe He still wants to heal people today."

"He certainly healed me!" Anthony beamed.

Early the next morning I was off to the other side of Pune to meet Deepak Tribhuvan of Prison Fellowship in India. My interest in Prison Fellowship started when I heard Charles Colson during one of his visits to England. He had been a legal aide to President Nixon during the Watergate affair, and was subsequently imprisoned for related offences. But during this time he committed his life to Jesus Christ, and he came out of prison a new man, determined to devote himself to prisoners and their need of Jesus Christ.

Prison Fellowship quickly spread from the U.S.A. to countries all over the world. Christians in India took up the challenge. Some had already been involved in prison work. Others, like Deepak Tribhuvan, were surprised to find themselves in such an unlikely setting.

"When Charles Colson came to Pune," Deepak told me, "he spoke at St. Xavier's Catholic Church. His theme was *reconciliation:* between Protestants and Catholics, between prisoners and the public, but especially between God and man."

It's this role of reconciliation to which Deepak is committed. And it's this vision that takes him into prisons throughout Maharastra, including the Central Prison, Yervada, the largest in the country.

Deepak was born and brought up in Pune and was in Wadia College, studying for an Arts degree, when a Pentecostal Christian by the name of Prasad began to visit his home. Deepak said: "I was searching for something real, and I had a growing sense of discomfort and unhappiness. It was easy at this stage to go drinking with my friends, but I knew this would not answer my problems."

Mr. Prasad took an interest in the restless young student. He tried to encourage him, and frequently prayed for him and spoke about the Bible. One day in 1973 Deepak walked out of the house in a very depressed frame of mind. He was so fed up with life that he thought seriously about suicide. Skipping his college classes he just roamed the streets, pondering what to do next. He felt so unimportant, so insignificant! It seemed as if no one cared.

He began to pray: "God, I've come to the stage where I'm going to take a drastic step. If You're real, show me!"

He retraced his steps and found himself back in front of his own house. With a heavy heart, he opened the door and went inside. Mr. Prasad was there again. Deepak sat down and observed the visitor as he opened his Bible and began to speak:

> Taste and see that the Lord is good,
> blessed is the man who takes refuge in
> Him.
> ...those who fear Him lack nothing.
> ...those who seek the Lord lack no good
> thing.
>
> (Ps. 34:8-10)

"Taste and see," Mr. Prasad kept saying. Deepak was listening intently to every word. Each one seemed to be making contact with a corresponding need in his life. Before the night was up Deepak realised that it wasn't Mr. Prasad only who was speaking to him - it was God! He prayed and gave his life to Christ.

"The next day as I went down the street to return to Wadia College I felt like leaping for joy," he told me. "God had given me that much peace!" Deepak soon realised that what had happened to him was the 'new birth' mentioned in John's Gospel. He had previously considered himself a Christian, but now he knew that a true Christian was 'born of the Spirit, not of the flesh'.

After completing his studies at Wadia College, Deepak began to pray for a born-again Christian wife. When he met Purnima, he believed she was God's choice for him. Unfortunately, his parents were not satisfied and did not approve of his decision. They had not been happy with his frequent church-going and his interest in Christian work. Although he retained a secular job, working for the government, his parents thought he should be out enjoying himself instead of going to church all the time!

Deepak, on the other hand, felt drawn to an even deeper involvement in Christian work. He thought perhaps God had a special task for him. Sometimes, at weekends, he'd go to one of Pune's slum districts and mingle with the impoverished people there. He and a few friends would take a megaphone and some musical instruments and hold a small meeting in the street.

Deepak became very soft-hearted. If he heard about a crime, tears would flow. He often prayed and wept before the Lord for those who were in trouble. But how could he do anything? "Whenever I read about a murderer in the newspaper," he said, "I wanted so much to see him and tell him about Jesus! I'd pray: 'Lord, You are a sovereign God: please put me in the place where I can contact such men.'"

In September 1981 Deepak felt that God was saying, "You don't have to look for criminals in the slums. They're all concentrated in one place: the prisons. Go and visit them there."

That was a new and awsome thought! He had no such contacts or training, and one Christian he approached for advice discouraged him, saying, "You won't get permission to do that sort of work."

Nevertheless, he went to the prison authorities and asked to speak to the superintendent of the prison. "I was terrified," he confessed. "But when I got to his door, I felt strangely at peace."

He told the Hindu superintendent: "God has given me a vision to pray for prisoners, and also to speak to them." He boldly suggested that he'd like to hold a meeting and tell the prisoners what Jesus had done for him. The superintendent was impressed and said: "What you are doing is a very good thing! Even I believe in Jesus Christ." Deepak was told to file an application. To his great joy, permission was granted two days later!

"I was very excited the first time," he told me. "There were seven hundred prisoners sitting there!" Deepak opened his talk by asking them: "How many of you have heard of Jesus Christ?" Only five prisoners raised their hands. Undaunted, he spoke of the love of God, and how much God loved them right then and there. He said that God wanted to forgive them, that although He hated sin, He loved the sinner! He told them how Jesus came down from heaven as a token of God's love.

"It was the first time anyone had told them that," Deepak said. "After the meeting fifty prisoners came to see me. They had all sorts of problems:

'My family lives far away and they are not being looked after.'

'How can I find peace in my heart?'

'Is it possible for me to change?'

'Some prison officials are so cruel.'

'I can't bear all the fighting.'

"Some came forward and wept like a child," Deepak said. "You could tell that God was speaking to them from that first meeting."

During Deepak's second visit to the prison he was permitted to go to the solitary confinement block. One of the prisoners who accepted a Gideon's New Testament at that time was a young man named Charan Singh.

'One of the most troublesome in the prison' was the superintendent's description of him. He had served ten years of a forty-six year sentence, and with fights and escape attempts to his 'credit' there was little hope of time off for good behaviour!

But as he began to read the New Testament for the first time, he realised what a sinner he was. When he read the Crucifixion story, he wept uncontrollably, realising that Jesus had died for *his* sins.

"That was five years ago," Deepak said, "and now Paul Charan Singh preaches boldly to all the prisoners, and even to the authorities! It is probable that he will be released soon, and he wants to return to the Punjab and take the gospel to prisoners there. It's too bad you don't read Hindi," Deepak told me with a smile. "Recently he has written his testimony - twenty-two pages of it - in Hindi!"

TWENTY ONE

Carey's legacy

Expect great things from God...
attempt great things for God.

William Carey

Pune is no longer the 'city of Rajneesh'. It is the city where Union Biblical Seminary sits on a twenty-two acre plateau overlooking Bibwevadi on the southern part of Pune. The tall cross suspended over the auditorium can be seen for miles around, and marks the spot where young people learn and train and then go out to every corner of India, to serve Jesus Christ and their fellow countrymen.

It was already very hot when the car climbed steeply up the winding mountain road. I saw the cross high above us but the path was no longer visible past the jagged rocks. Gradually the narrow road levelled off and there beyond a pair of gates were a well-shaped cluster of buildings flanking a central edifice.

This four year old campus, carved out of the side of a mountain, didn't have that hollow, homeless feeling of so many new institutions. Of course UBS had its roots elsewhere, at Yavatmal, in Central Maharastra, where it remained for thirty years, before being transplanted to the Pune countryside. But there was already a wonderful feeling of continuity about the place, amongst the clusters of students, in the quiet library and bustling dining hall, even outside amongst the workmen who were now erecting further buildings. I felt it in the near-empty auditorium, as my guide Sunny and I stood there quietly.

And then, as if he read my thoughts, Sunny motioned me up to an old wooden pulpit on the platform. "This was a pulpit William Carey used when he preached in Serampore," he said.

My hand instinctively went out to touch the darkened wood - to think of that remarkable man standing behind this very pulpit! William Carey had been my particular hero since my conversion thirty years before. That poor, self-taught village boy from England sailed for India after countless difficulties and supported his family and colleagues himself while preaching, teaching, translating and publishing grammars and Bibles in about forty Oriental languages. He promoted reforms in India that resulted in the 1801 law prohibiting the sacrificing of children, and the 1829 law abolishing *sati*, the burning of widows on their husband's funeral pyres.

But even as I reverently touched that time-worn wood, I knew his real legacy was the lives of Christians throughout India - people like Pervez Sethna, one of the UBS students who told me his story as we sat in the quiet chapel between classes.

Pervez came from a Parsi family in Agra where his father's family was in the wine and liquor wholesale business. However, his father 'converted' to Christianity in 1957 in order to marry and that severed most links with the Parsi community. In 1970 the family moved to Lucknow and the parents came into contact with Christians from a group of Bakht Singh assembly believers. First his father and a year later his mother committed their lives to Christ and were baptised. But Pervez found all this religious ceremony tiresome and refused to attend the baptism. "Go ahead and get drowned in the river!" he said angrily.

It was not just his parents' newly found faith that was widening a gap between them. Pervez began to neglect his studies, and by the age of fourteen had rebelled against any sort of authority, was smoking, using drugs and had taken up with bad company.

The following year, due to his poor record at school, his principal refused to allow him to sit for his final exams. Pervez didn't care: it gave him the opportunity to run away from home, and he cycled off to an unsuspecting relative over fifty miles away. He remained there until his photo appeared in a newspaper and an announcement was made on TV. When his family learnt where he'd been hiding, he was forced to return home to Lucknow. But he came back more hardened than ever. "I won't do anything I don't want to do," he announced defiantly to his worried parents. He kept his word: quarrels at home, nights out with bad companions, minimum effort at school. Life lived on his terms only.

One morning in October there was a terrible row at home. His parents went off to work and his sister left for school. Pervez had only enough money for a ticket to Cawnpore, so he purchased this and got on the train. But he didn't get off until Bombay.

Pervez spent the first night on the platform, without money or food. In the early hours, the police moved him on. He began to walk through Bombay the following day, sleeping on the pavement in dirty jeans and soiled shirt. For three days he walked and slept, and had only a few scraps of food. He still had his pride. "I wasn't going to stoop to ask anyone for help," he told me. "I thought I was still my own man!"

He found a job in a small cafe, picking up the dishes and washing them in a cramped kitchen. He was glad of the job and assumed that after a day's work he could get something substantial to eat. He carried on working for seven hours.

"Can I have something to eat? he asked the boss finally.

"No!"

In his fatigue and hunger he stumbled and collided with another person. "Take him outside and beat him!" the boss ordered, and hands grabbed him and flung him outside. After giving him a thorough beating, they told him: "Get lost!" Pervez stumbled off, pride and body wounded, hungrier than ever. He was not yet sixteen years old. He thought to himself, "Surely I can do better than this!"

After he was tossed out, a nearby restauranteur observed the miserable boy and had pity on him. Pervez admitted that he had run away and that he was from Lucknow. Amazingly the man was also from Lucknow, and he too had run away as a youth fourteen years earlier! He gave Pervez some food and allowed him to take a bath and wash his shirt, letting him stay there the night and even giving him five rupees. And he told Pervez that he'd see about finding a job for him!

But despite such a promising start to the friendship, no job was offered. Pervez hung around the restaurant for three days, again without food or money. Finally he concluded he might as well finish it all. What good was it to live in this way? There was a close friend of his father who lived in Bombay. Perhaps, thought Pervez, he could pay him a final visit. He climbed the steps, a very dirty and scruffy young man, but when the door opened, Pervez was welcomed inside. The man gave him a meal and clothes, and they spent the afternoon in pleasant conversation.

There was a knock on the door and when the man opened it, Pervez' father was standing there! He had come to Bombay to look for his son, and in his arms he carried a parcel of clothing. His father spoke so lovingly to him that Pervez felt too guilty to speak. He returned to Lucknow with his father on November 7, 1974, but the truce was short-lived. Pervez soon drifted back to his old friends and began smoking and drinking with them. "If you say anything to me," Pervez would threaten his father, "I'll run away again!"

During the next few years, sometimes he'd hear his father praying for him. That infuriated him most of all. These praying Christians, crowding in on him! Why didn't they just leave him alone? He was smoking heavily now, and took hashish whenever he could. He often had headaches and would sometimes fall over. When his pains became serious he agreed to go to a neuro-surgeon, who suspected a tumour. When he began to have convulsions, he was taken to hospital and given a battery of tests. The doctors were baffled: he was not responding to any treatment, and sometimes he'd be in continuous pain for eight or nine hours a time.

"In October 1979 I was at the crossroads of my life," Pervez told me. "My mother and dad lost almost all hope. But mother believed that if only I would read some Scriptures I could be healed. And so she put a New Testament in my hospital room." One afternoon as he lay there, Pervez picked it up. It made him think of the good life he used to have. He had once represented the state in softball, and excelled at sport in college. "What have I done to myself?" he reflected. "I can't even sit up without aid!"

Pervez opened the New Testament and began to read parts of John's Gospel:

> Do not let your hearts be troubled.
> Trust in God; trust also in Me...
> You may ask Me for anything in My name,
> and I will do it...
> Peace I leave with you;
> My peace I give you.
> I do not give to you as the world gives.
> Do not let your hearts be troubled
> and do not be afraid...
> Greater love has no one than this,
> that He lay down His life for His friends....
>
> (from John 14 and 15)

How loving Jesus was - how gentle with His disciples! "There might still be meaning in life for me," Pervez thought.

One day a Christian friend came to visit and asked, "Pervez, do you think Jesus can heal you?" Pervez was weary and miserable and wanted the person to go, so it seemed simpler to agree with him.

"Well then," the visitor was emboldened, "will you pray now?"

So Pervez had to agree. "Lord," he prayed aloud, "I do not know how to pray. I am so tired. Please give me one more life."

As he prayed, Pervez felt a gentle pressure on his head, and also one on his heart! As that pressure was released, something seemed to flee! After the friend left, Pervez drifted into a deep sleep. When he awoke, he was free of all pain!

"Jesus healed me!" he announced to his puzzled parents when they came again. They looked at each other and then at the pathetic figure lying in the bed. Had this illness now affected his mind?

"I will take no more medicines," he insisted. "I believe

the Lord is healing me."

In the days to come, Pervez picked up the New Testament frequently, and found wonderful comfort in the little book:

> You did not choose Me, but I chose you
> and appointed you to go and bear fruit,
> fruit that will last...
>
> (John 15:16)

"That's what I want," he said to Jesus then. "Even in physical infirmity, I'll live for You. I give my whole life to You." And he confessed all of his sins to his new Lord and Saviour.

The doctors came to study their patient more closely. Then the psychiatrist arrived! Pervez told them all, "Jesus healed me!" and they laughed. He could not even walk by himself!

"Father, I want to go to church," he said when his parents returned. "I know the Lord will touch me there." So the family took him to their church, Bethel Fellowship in Lucknow. Friends saw a different young man from the one they'd seen before. It was not only the illness that had softened and humbled him; the old defiance had gone. Pervez began to enter into the worship, with its enthusiastic singing and clapping. Suddenly his pain returned and the agony was terrible. When the pastor saw what had happened he stopped the singing, took out a small bottle of ointment and anointed Pervez' head. And everyone prayed for his healing.

It was the last time he was to suffer in that way. When he returned to the hospital for further tests, the doctors could find nothing wrong with him.

"Now I had fully decided to live for God," he told me. "I read the Bible avidly and realised I should be baptised. And on December 9, 1979 I was baptised in water. I continued to study the Bible, knowing I had a lot to learn."

One day Pervez realised he had not yet asked forgiveness from his parents and sister for all those years of unhappiness he'd caused them. Like the prodigal, Pervez said,

"Father, I have sinned against heaven and
against you. I am no longer worthy to be
called your son...."

(Luke 15:21)

But, like the forgiving father in that parable, Pervez'
father had already forgiven him.

TWENTY TWO

The vision

I stand under the golden canopy of
Thine evening sky and I lift
my eager eyes to Thy face.

Rabrindrath Tagore
Gitanjali

We were speeding along on the country roads that morning, with Pune city at our backs. Our destination was Kedgeon, the home of Mukti Mission. The roads were, as usual, pitted and rough, and the ride was bumpy.

My driver brought a friend along, an amazing-looking fellow with an intricate pattern chalked out between his eyes, a multi-coloured, angular version of the Hindu woman's *bottu*. Had he spoken English, I would have been bold enough to ask him about it. But neither he nor my driver spoke anything but Marati, so I was none the wiser. Nevertheless they turned and smiled at me regularly and cheerfully, stopping only once to scowl when I got them outside for a photo. Perhaps a smile *en camera* is bad luck?

The friend was deposited at a small village halfway through the journey, and the rest of the ride was taken in silence. We drove through canopies of banyans and past a procession of ox carts. The animals' horns were painted red or gold, the tips festooned with bells or tassels. There was a marble quarry in the middle of nowhere, where men in loin cloths were painstakingly moving the beautiful lumps of stone.

Then we came upon a 'village' of brick ovens, neatly arranged in steaming pyramids like a housing estate with chimneys smoking. Again workmen - and women - were carrying bricks and cement, feeding the ovens to cook the bricks, pulling out the finished products and keeping the fires burning.

And then we were in Kedgeon, and I thrilled to see the

wooden archway announcing MUKTI MISSION atop the green-painted latticed fencing. The path was overhung with blossom, and I walked underneath the foliage into the dusty but neatly swept compound.

I confess to an elation equal to the one I felt when I first came upon the Taj Mahal. Here was history, too! But this place was a monument to love of a different kind: the love of a woman for the unfortunates and outcastes of society, a love only made possible through Jesus who loved them first.

Dr. Sheila Gupta was there to greet me: grey hair loosely tied, a strong though gentle face, a white doctor's coat over a simple white cotton sari. We walked down a long porch into her neat and simply furnished quarters. She had put aside her work for the day to devote herself to me. Now I too was a recipient of the selfless dedication found at Mukti - and shown to any wayfarers whatever their rank or situation.

Mukti Mission is known the world over as the home of Pandita Ramabai, a remarkable Brahmin Hindu born in 1858. Both her parents died of starvation in the famine of 1876-77 and within a few years she was married and then widowed, when her Bengali husband died of cholera. She began long pilgrimages in a search for peace for her soul, and finally discovered the living Jesus Christ through some Anglican community sisters. The Mukti Mission was founded because of her love for the Saviour and her concern for girls and women in need.

In recent years Dr. Sheila Gupta has become the resident doctor and superintendent, overseeing a community of more than five hundred women and children, some of whom arrived homeless, or orphaned, or mentally or physically disabled. But no one needing help is excluded from Mukti.

We talked together for an hour and then Dr. Gupta went outside with a tray of food for my driver, who was stretched out asleep inside the sun-baked Ambassador. He was not expecting the generous food and drink, and certainly not expecting it to be served by the superintendent!

Finally we sat down to lunch ourselves. "When I was ten

years old," she told me, "my mother died. My father, a government medical doctor, was transferred to an area in the Himalayas, and to unburden my sorrow I decided to go on a fast and a pilgrimage. It was Krishna's birthday, and I set out to climb to the temple on the top of a five thousand feet mountain.

"As I walked along I grew tired and hungry. There was snow on the ground, and I instinctively reached out to scoop some up. But then I remembered my mother's warning that one who breaks a fast brings evil upon himself. And I withheld my hand. Finally I reached the top, excited at the prospect of seeing the god and unburdening my grief to him.

"But I reached the 'temple' - a crumbling stone porch - and there was no god there! Just a slab of stone and an old priest who was indifferent to my presence." She retraced her steps and went home broken-hearted, her sorrow greater than ever.

Sheila had wanted to be a doctor since the age of four. She studied first of all at the famous Isobel Thoburn College and then entered medical school in Agra at the age of nineteen. While a student she was taken by her father to a famous temple, reached only after many hours of walking. They arrived mid-afternoon and Sheila, eager for her *darshan*, her glimpse of the god, hurried to the room where the deity was kept. To her dismay, she found a big lock on the door. Finally a keeper appeared. "You can't view the god now," he said. "It's time for him to sleep."

Sheila was amazed. "How can the creator of the universe need some sleep?" she wondered. It was the beginning of her doubts. There seemed to be something seriously wrong with the religion she followed.

After completing her training Sheila wanted to do post-graduate work, as her ambition was to become a head of department or professor of gynaecology and obstetrics. She applied twice to the famous Christian Medical College in Vellore, but was unable to secure a place. Suddenly in October 1954 a letter arrived, telling her to come at once. In those first weeks at the college when her surroundings were still unfamiliar, she would step out on to her balcony and look up at the hills, remembering her childhood.

Now at this most successful time of her life, when she should be proud and happy with her situation, a melancholy mood crept over her.

"At that time I did not relate my depression to any spiritual problem," she told me. "I assumed it was just the adjustment to a new place and a different language and culture."

She thought she might find relief working extra hard, but the restlessness increased and she had trouble sleeping. Hour after hour she stood on the balcony, gazing out at the hills and up at the stars.

One night as she was looking over the hills, she suddenly saw the Lord Jesus on the cross, and became very frightened. "Why should I see this?" she wondered. "He doesn't mean anything to me!" She didn't dare tell anyone about this strange incident, but the vision continued. Night after night, each time she walked out on the balcony, there was the Lord Jesus appearing before her on a cross!

One afternoon Sheila noticed amongst her books a neglected Bible, given her once by a Christian friend. Where should she begin to read? It fell open at the story of Christ's trial.

Sheila's tears dropped on the pages of the Bible as she read. "Why should I weep," she wondered, "when Jesus doesn't mean anything to me?"
Nevertheless she read on:

> Then Pilate took Jesus and had Him flogged. The soldiers twisted together a crown of thorns and put it on His head. They clothed Him in a purple robe and went up to Him again and again, saying "Hail, king of the Jews!" And they struck Him in the face. Once more Pilate came out and said to the Jews, "Look, I am bringing Him out to you to let you know that I find no basis for a charge against

> Him." When Jesus came out wearing the
> crown of thorns and the purple robe,
> Pilate said to them, "Here is the man!" As
> soon as the chief priests and their officials
> saw Him, they shouted, "Crucify! Crucify!"
>
> (John 19:1-6)

Sheila was again moved to tears. She felt compelled to read on:

> Carrying His own cross, He went out to the
> 'place of the skull' (which in Aramaic is
> called Golgotha). Here they crucified
> Him, and with Him two others - one on
> each side and Jesus in the middle. Pilate
> had a notice prepared and fastened to the
> cross. It read: JESUS OF NAZARETH,
> THE KING OF THE JEWS.
>
> (John 19:17-19)

She closed the Bible and tried to put that dreadful picture out of her mind. But in spite of herself she picked up the Bible the next night - and the next - and re-read those passages. But she told no one about it.

One day a friend, an Australian physiotherapist, quoted from the Bible to her:

> Here I am! I stand at the door and knock.
> If anyone hears My voice and opens the
> door, I will come in and eat with him, and
> he with Me.
>
> (Rev. 3:20)

Sheila objected to this - she thought the young woman was trying to convert her.

But a night or two later, she heard a loud knock on her door. At first she thought it was the ward aid, calling her for duty. But there was no one there, and she remembered the verse her friend had quoted.

It was Easter Week 1955, and every day that week, sometimes in chapel, sometimes on the radio, Sheila heard,

> When I survey the wondrous cross
> On which the Prince of Glory died,
> My richest gain I count but loss
> And pour contempt on all my pride...

The words and the tune went round and round in her head.

"At the back of my mind I was weighing them up: Krishna on the one hand, Jesus on the other. All that week the turmoil went on. Sometimes I'd decide I'd have nothing to do with Jesus Christ. But still the battle raged."

One evening she was sitting on the terrace, looking out over the hills, and once more she saw Christ hanging on a cross. "I had never known peace before," she said. "That night, when my heart broke, I asked the Lord Jesus to come in to my life. The vision faded then, and a great peace came over me. I went back to my room and wrote what I'd done in the back of my Bible. It was 9.15 p.m., April 4 1955."

Soon after her conversion Sheila sensed that God was giving her two conditions for her life: that she must obey Him without question, and that she must allow Him to plan her path.

Brother Bakht Singh came to Vellore, and Sheila attended the meetings. He spoke about baptism, and principles of church life. Sheila was eager to learn. She thought of baptism as a step to take at some future date. But when she was reading the Bible, she came upon a verse that startled her:

> Why do you call Me, "Lord, Lord", and do
> not do what I say?
>
> (Luke 6:46)

She immediately contacted her friends at the assembly, and Brother Bakht Singh baptised her that same month.

Her first temptation came soon enough. She was offered

a scholarship to study in America, but declined it, knowing it was not right for her at that time. She continued with her research, and began to study tuberculosis in women. "I had come a complete revolution now," she smiled. "Instead of wanting higher degrees, I wanted to work in a village hospital somewhere."

A missionary came to Vellore and spoke about Mukti Mission, where the staff were praying for a resident doctor. Until that time, Sheila had never heard of Pandita Ramabai and her early role in improving the lot of India's women.

Sheila was a new Christian, inexperienced in prayer. But with childlike simplicity she brought her needs to God each day. For nine months she prayed about this question of her future work. One morning the word MUKTI flashed through her mind. When she picked up her *Daily Light*, the portion read:

> See, I have placed before you an open
> door that no one can shut.
>
> (Rev. 3:8)

"Lord, are you calling me to go to Mukti?" she asked with some amazement..

Brother Bakht Singh returned for a series of meetings, and Sheila sought his advice about going to Mukti. He felt peace in his heart about it, and she took this as confirmation.

He told her how, in 1938, he had visited Mukti himself. There were close to one thousand women and children there and for three weeks hundreds of women met every night for an all-night prayer meeting.

"It was because of the travailing prayer of those women," he told her then, "that we were enabled to start Jeho-Shamma in Madras."

Sheila never forgot that story. "When a group of Christians pray," she said, "it can affect the life, work or safety of someone far away."

Dr. Sheila moved to Mukti Mission as superintendent in February 1957: not only to work as a doctor, but to learn discipleship in the Lord's school. Early on she learnt to take the step of faith. That year she suffered from a painful dental cyst. Her Muslim doctor showed her the X-ray, which indicated the need for an operation. But her reading that morning suggested another course of action:

> Fight the good fight of the faith. Take hold of the eternal life to which you were called when you made your good confession in the presence of many witnesses.
>
> (1 Tim. 6:12)

What if a larger issue was at stake? The question was no sooner formed than three things happened simultaneously. The Lord Jesus appeared at the side of her bed, reached over and touched her face. The growth in her jaw broke, and pus flowed from the painful infection. And she cried out: "The Lord Jesus has done the operation!"

That was only a foretaste of the steps of faith she would take in other - more difficult - circumstances. But it was an illustration of the faith principle.

He also taught her lessons of relinquishment. "I was a very self-assertive person," Dr. Sheila smiled, "always ready to fight for my rights. It was very difficult to be in situations where silence was the only course, even when one felt one's way was right."

It was a process she described as 'breaking and cutting and pruning': a work which the Christian cannot and does not do upon himself but which he must be willing for the Master to do.

In 1960 her Saviour clearly asked her to 'love Me as your heavenly Bridegroom.' She knelt down at once, and said her marriage vows. That same day, she read in Isaiah:

> For your Maker is your husband;
> the Lord Almighty is His name.
> The Holy One of Israel is your Redeemer;
> He is called the God of all the earth.
>
> (Isa. 54:5)

"For this you need a call from God," she told me. "Some Christians remain single, and then later comes frustration and longing for marriage. But when God gives the call to celibacy, He gives enabling grace."

It was a surprise to her in 1962 when the way was opened for her to go to Moody Bible Institute in the U.S.A. She felt that God had already led her away from all that. But renunciation can take many forms: one may be obliged to return to a position previously abandoned, and sometimes this is the most difficult step of all.

But her two years in America proved to be a very valuable part of her training, and she learnt to trust God as provider. "God met every need during those years at Moody," she said. "I didn't need to take a *paisa* from my father.

"The most sacred and vital ministry of the Christian," she told me, "is to keep the devotional fire burning. All through the ages people have found it easier to make an external show of good works or sacrifices than to seek repentance and undergo an inner cleansing. But God isn't fooled by this! He seeks the true sacrifice: an intensity of love and devotion that illuminates our lives and work from the inside out. Often our initial love is intense. But then some get side-tracked, or grow cold, even though they continue to work for Him." In the book of Revelation Jesus warns about this:

> Yet I have this against you: You have
> forsaken your first love. Remember the
> height from which you have fallen: Repent
> and do the things you did at first.
>
> (Rev. 2:4-5)

In recent years God has moved Dr. Sheila out of Mukti for periods of ministry. The Mission continues to be her base, but God has opened many doors throughout India and neighbouring countries for her to share the message of Jesus Christ.

We went for a tour of Mukti Mission. There was Pandita Ramabai's room, just as she had left it: her bed, her desk, the Marati Bible which she translated, along with other books and grammars. A display showed her many activities, including the way she taught illiterate village women how to typeset and produce the many pieces of literature and books on the four printing presses she bought.

"Sometimes she dressed as an outcaste," Dr. Sheila said, "just to go out and rescue women and children in danger.

"This is where the fire of the Lord fell in 1938," Dr. Sheila told me, as we entered the pavillion. "The benefits of that revival were felt in many parts of India. Some of the young women experienced an outpouring of the Holy Spirit and went into towns and villages throughout the state. Many, many people came to know Jesus at that time. One of those girls is an old lady now living at Mukti. She was rescued by Pandidta Ramabai in the early years of this century, and went out to preach in the villages for many years. Would you like to meet her?"

Manchi Akka - 'the old one' - was curled up on her bed asleep. She jumped up at once, with a bright and toothless smile. Her size was that of a young girl, but she might have been one hundred. No one knew her age. She was brought to Mukti at the age of nine or ten, and her years of preaching in the villages had brought many to know Jesus.

Now Dr. Sheila sat with her arm around her, asking her my questions in Marati. Such a fragile wrinkled old body, but her voice was so loud and clear that it echoed along the stone floors and into other rooms. Manchi told us how 'Mother' Ramabai was very strict with the girls, but would enter into the punishment herself. "If she disciplined a girl by withholding food," Manchi said, "then Mother herself would not eat! She was very stern about lies or any wrong-doing. That's why people say 'give us the women of her time'!"

Manchi loved to reminisce about 'Mother' Ramabai: about the clothes she gave out at Christmastime, her constant love to all her 'children', and her saintly life in pointing people to Jesus.

Something was happening to me these past few days, I thought as the car pulled away from Mukti Mission and headed back to Pune. Perhaps it began when I was sitting in the UBS chapel with Pervez Sethna. As tears ran down his face, he had told me how one wandering and wayward Parsi discovered God's forgiveness. That was when I too had to weep; something seemed to break within me. The next day it happened again in the flat of an elderly Christian as I watched that dear man's face while he told of the difficulties that are part of the Christian's walk. Today, the moment I walked through the Mukti gates I was again deeply moved.

"The fire is burning," Dr. Sheila had said at one point, "and I cannot keep quiet...."

As we sped homeward along the rough road I knew it was her devotional fire that challenged me. Moments later as I looked out of my window, I again saw the brickmakers, still busy with their tasks. The fires were still burning, the bricks being moulded for tomorrow's family dwellings. Those workmen had to be vigilant and ensure that the fires did not die down.

I remembered Rev. Augustine Salins, India's beloved 'weeping prophet', who was preparing a sermon with the text:

> The fire must be kept burning on the altar
> continuously; it must not go out.
>
> (Lev. 6:13)

He didn't live long enough to preach that sermon but until the day he died, 'the fire was ever burning' on his altar for Jesus.

I left the following day for my last stop before the final flight to London. It was a long queue, as usual, with a surplus of officials making a major production of a simple formality for reasons known only to themselves. I was worn out already, and we had twelve hours of flying ahead of us.

Suddenly a group of *Hare Krishna* devotees appeared on my right, Western youths in orange robes and shaved heads.

There were strange markings on their foreheads. And they spoke with *London* accents! I turned to my left, and watched three stout ladies in long white gowns with medallions on their breasts, bearing photos of a guru. They too were Westerners, heading for the U.K. I turned to the man behind me. His luggage tag showed he was a clergyman. How wonderful to find a kindred spirit!

"Isn't it awful," I asked him, "to think of what's being brouhgt back into Britain?"

He looked at me cooly. "Oh I don't know," he said. "I think it enriches us."

TWENTY THREE

Not by our own power

> *Why do you look so*
> *earnestly on us? As though by our*
> *own power or holiness we had*
> *made this man to walk?*
>
> **Acts 3:12**

It was early morning in Calcutta but already very hot. Sister Martha walked through the gates of *Prem Dan*, the disused factory given over to the work of the Sisters of the Missionaries of Charity. Another day to care for the sick and homeless - some in conditions so desperate that a year before she couldn't have looked at them! Already people were sitting or lying everywhere, some waiting for medicines or food, others to have dressings changed on infected limbs. A woman who'd been attacked by rats stood impassively to one side. A child with a worm-eaten body was held by his mother.

Sister Martha thought with a smile of how she had recoiled when she first heard of this place. Her sister had entered Mother Teresa's Missionaries of Charity two years before and her letters home terrified Martha. Brought up in a pleasant corner of Goa, she had seen shanty towns here and there but did not know what went on inside. She had attended the convent on the other side of the city, where there were trees and gardens on the side of a hill. After that she had studied medicine at the blossom-covered college behind the convent. A pleasant and rewarding career as a doctor awaited her.

But those dreadful letters! Each one, full of horrific descriptions, ended: "Martha! There's a place for you here." That disturbed her most of all. Not that she did not love God. She was brought up in a devout Catholic home, with parents who lived their faith as well as taught it. But she was a vivacious girl, in love with life. She had many friends - and admirers - and a commitment to a religious community did not fit in with her plans.

Then something began to happen within Martha herself. Somewhere between January and June of 1974 she became aware of a greater love within her for Jesus, eclipsing all other relationships, friendships and loves. As the year wore on, she realised He had become the most important person in her life. Gradually she knew that her only desire was to do what He wanted.

It was about that time that she read her sister's letters more carefully. They no longer held a threat. She wrote to Mother Teresa, offering herself to the Missionaries of Charity, but assuming that if accepted, she'd complete her studies and qualify in medicine before joining. But Mother Teresa wrote back: "Come at once!" So she did.

Now passing through the gates, Sister Martha noticed a commotion nearby. A crowd had gathered round someone who was screaming loudly. As she pressed in she saw a boy of about eighteen, naked, throwing himself on the ground and shouting. He was spitting and cursing, and he flung aside any piece of cloth offered to cover himself. A man in great distress spied the sister and rushed to her. He cast himself on the ground and caught at her feet. "Oh please," he cried, "do something for my son! He is possessed by a devil and needs your help! I have brought him all this way to you."

The sister was frightened. Sights of death and dying had become almost commonplace to her by now, but what could she do to help this tormented youth? With the father still clinging to her feet, she prayed, "Oh Jesus, help him!" Sister Martha hurried off to her superior and asked permission to keep the boy on the premises for a brief time. This given, she managed to take him to a quiet place away from the curious crowds. Taking some holy water, she put it on his head and blessed him. As she did so she remembered the anguish of his father, the desperate look on his face. "Jesus can do it," she thought, and turned it into a prayer.

Within a few days the father returned to visit his son. What he found was a clean and smiling youth, no longer tormented, 'clothed, and in his right mind'. "What have you done?" the father cried out to the sister. Again he grasped her feet but this time out of gratitude and joy.

"Get up!" she urged him. "I have done nothing! It was Jesus Who healed him." And she tried to explain about the Great Physician who wants to heal our bodies, minds and spirits. But the father kept looking at his restored son, weeping, "Thank you...thank you..."

Within the week, they returned to *Prem Dan*. The father brought back his well-dressed son and urged him, "Come and thank the sister."

Sister Martha reminded them both that God *alone* should be thanked, for it was He Who healed and delivered the boy. And she told them more about Jesus.

A month later the father again appeared at *Prem Dan* and asked for Sister Martha. He was holding two plump and beautiful birds, a cock and a hen. "I have come to tell you more about my son," the man beamed at the young nun. "He is working so well on the farm every day and is now a wonderful boy! And," he added proudly, "I have brought these gifts for you, to thank you for what you have done!"

"But I told you," the sister said, "you must not thank me. I could not possibly accept these, for I did nothing to deserve them. Offer your thanks to God Who has done this wonderful thing for you."

And she then told him how Jesus once healed a man similarly tormented. Like the man in the story, she told him to go home and tell people that God had healed his son. She watched him turn and walk away, still carrying the cock and the hen.

I first heard about Sister Martha a few years ago in Bombay, as her mother was seated next to me at a Christian fellowship dinner. From that evening I wanted to meet her. It seemed unlikely that this would happen: she was first in Calcutta and then later in Bangladesh working with refugees and abandoned children.

But God loves to give gifts to His children, like my unexpected visit to a Missionaries of Charity home, where

Sister Martha 'just happened' to be staying.

"What effect did that boy's healing have on your life?" I asked the beautiful young sister that afternoon as we sat together in a small side room.

"I suppose from then on I've believed even more in the miraculous," she said. "And so often, when we least expect it, it happens! When we just abandon a problem into His hands and say 'Do what You think best', He often surprises us with something wonderful!"

"Her face is so radiant," I said to a helper as I was leaving. "So Christ-like!"

"Yes, it is," he agreed. "Sister Martha is in charge of all our postulants. It's such a wise choice. After they've spent one month with her, their faces are like that, too!"

TWENTY FOUR

The mystery doctor

From now on I will tell of you new things,
of hidden things unknown to you.

Isaiah 48:6

I first met the doctor in a mission in the Frasertown district of Bangalore. It was a strangely moving experience and I found myself much affected by this gentle, dignified man from the Burmese border. His grandfather, who had been a headhunter in a remote mountain tribe, was met by a misisonary and became a follower of Jesus Christ.

In a quiet and unspectacular way the doctor spoke of the battle still being waged against the ancient spirits - not just in the isolated regions from which he came, but in villages, towns and cities throughout India.

"The trouble with modern man," he said, "is that he thinks civilisation has destroyed the dark and evil spirit world. But it hasn't. It has only managed to dress up the beast, clothe him and refine him, hoping he won't be recognised. But he's still there."

He pointed out that each country in its spiritual restlessness reaches out for a 'something' beyond its shores that might bring peace. Many Indians, sensing the futility of their own religious systems, have found in Western films and music a way of escape and are totally caught up in them.

"But such things haven't been enough for us in the West!" I reminded him. "Many of our people are heading to India to find what has eluded them."

"That's because they've rejected the light that has been available to them," he said. "You've had a Christian heritage for centuries. I believe it has been this that has given you order and justice."

It was to be more than four years before I met the doctor again. Repeated attempts to find out his name and whereabouts failed. Then unexpectedly, came a letter from a friend in Greece: "...There's someone you really should meet. His grandfather was a headhunter on the Burmese border. His name is Dr. Ben Wati."

It turned out that the doctor was due in England for a conference, so we were honoured to have him in our home. He began with his grandfather's story.

Odang Chetba ran out of his house to see what was happening. Coming up the hill were neighbouring tribesmen with murder in their eyes. They rushed forward and before the terrified villagers could defend themselves they seized a beautiful young girl whose hair reached down to her ankles. One moment she was screaming out: the next there was a flash of sunlight on the blade of the long machete, and the killers seized the severed head and rushed away in triumph.

What a bitter humiliation for the village which had been proud and unconquered for so many years! Odang Chetba resolved never to forget this. The other men were also outraged. They began to discuss strategy, determined to travel to the enemy village thirty miles distant, and take a head from one of the killers.

Meanwhile the British had come to the area and served warning on all the tribes that there was to be no more headhunting. It was outlawed and wrong-doers would be punished. But the village men continued to plan their attack. At the most auspicious moment, Odang Chetba and two other young men crept from the village and set out for their do-or-die mission. The British authorities meant little to them; their lives were controlled by the spirit world, and their fear of the evil spirits was greater than their fear of the white man's laws.

Odang returned to his tribe carrying the head of an enemy. Thus the murder of the young girl was avenged and honour restored to the village. His companions must have keenly felt his triumph because he named his first son 'one who is envied by his peers'. He became a leader and a spokesman in the village and head of the Jamir clan. His booming voice made everyone take notice. But then his name meant 'one who speaks clearly and forthrightly'.

Not long afterwards the British authorities learnt of the revenge killing and that Odang was responsible. He was taken from the village, tried, and sentenced to three years' imprisonment at Tezpur in Assam. During those years, with little to occupy his time, the prisoner learnt the Assamese language. This equipped him well for the future, because it was the language used by the British to communicate to the Naga tribes. On his release Odang was given a red blanket by the British, signifying his new role in acting as a link between the authorities and the tribesmen.

It was shortly after this that an American missionary couple, Dr. and Mrs. Clark, came to Nagaland. Dr. Clark moved amongst hill tribes never before touched by the Christian message. When tribesmen were willing to leave their old ways and become followers of Jesus Christ, they accompanied Dr. Clark as he walked to the next village. Thus nine neighbouring tribesmen - and one white man - ascended the hill to the Ao Nagas that day in 1875.

Dr. Clark came to a people full of fears and superstition. These were illiterate tribesmen and there was no written language. They were animists, who worshipped - and greatly feared - evil spirits, sacrificing animals to them. Headhunting was a means of showing bravery and requiting wrongs. There was great darkness and evil in their lives.

The people crowded round the strangers, wondering what brought them to their village. It was unusual for other Nagas to come in that way. Stranger still was the sight of Dr. Clark, standing in the clearing ready to speak. But first one of the visiting Nagas stepped forward.

"We also are with this man," he said. "We have listened to his words. What he says is true." Several others nodded and confirmed that they too were leaving the old ways to follow Jesus.

Odang Chetba listened as Dr. Clark began to speak. He described the fear that ruled their lives, he spoke about the vengeance they felt for their enemies and he talked about the wickedness that lived in their hearts. Odang had to admit that what he said was true. Then the man spoke of a

God unknown in the Naga hills who loved people so much, despite their wrong-doing, that He sent His only Son Jesus to die for them. And on the cross, this perfect Son of God said:

> Please forgive them, Father; they don't
> know what they're doing.

Then Dr. Clark took a long bamboo pole and laid it in front of him in the village square. Everyone stood in a wide circle watching.

"All of those who would like to turn from your old ways," said Dr. Clark, "who will stop worshipping evil spirits and who want to follow Jesus Christ Who died for your sins - you step across this bamboo pole to show you mean it."

Odang Chetba made a decision that day that changed his life, that of his children and his children's children, and the lives of many people in Nagaland. He moved forward and stepped over the bamboo pole.

Dr. Clark could not remain long in the village, but he taught Odang and the other new Christians many things and promised to return later. Soon Dr. Clark began to reduce their language to writing. After devising the alphabet he began to collect words for a dictionary, and then he started to translate the New Testament into the Ao Naga tongue.

The arrival of Christianity changed the village in many ways. Formerly there was no need to tell the time or know what day it was. Then they learnt that every seventh day was to be the one set aside for worshipping the true God, There would be meetings at two different times on that day. Thus a bamboo strip was hung prominently and marked into seven pieces. Each day a section would be cut off and when the final piece was the only one left, then it would be Sunday! A gong was placed outside the headman's thatched and bamboo house, and sometimes the children were permitted to strike it, to call the villagers to the meetings.

Odang's family experienced many changes. His seven children were now brought up in a Christian home and attended the mission school set up so that children could not only learn to read and write but learn portions of the Bible and how to live the Christian life. Odang's second son became one of the mission school teachers.

Many of his neighbours had also 'crossed the bamboo' when he did and were now living differently. The men lost their interest in drinking rice beer, and became more loving to their wives and children. They never again sacrificed animals to the spirits and they found that now there was no room in their hearts for hatred of their enemies.

When Odang was eighty years of age, he became gravely ill. His friends built his coffin and prepared for a Christian burial. But the old man recovered and ordered his sons to put the coffin inside his house. They carried it up the stairs of his raised thatch-and-bamboo dwelling and set it down in the room. He was proud of his new 'bench', the only piece of furniture in the room! It would also provide seating for guests who came to visit. And he discovered he could store his tools within the coffin, so it became a useful tool-box as well.

Odang Chetba lived for thirty more years and died at the age of one hundred and ten: an ex-headhunter who became a faithful follower of Jesus Christ.

TWENTY FIVE

Three wishes

*Delight yourself in the Lord
and He will give you
the desires of your heart.*

Psalm 37:4

"Come and play football!" the young boys cried to their friend, who was sweeping out his house.

Seven year old Ben looked hopefully at his mother, but she was adamant. "You cannot go," she said firmly, "until you finish your chores."

The boy turned back to his tasks, wishing that he had sisters to do this work like most of his friends. But he was the eldest of seven brothers and his work was not finished until he had tended the pigs and chickens that lived beneath the house, and then gathered some firewood for the evening meal.

Later Ben was seen wandering on the outskirts of the village collecting twigs and small branches, trying to imitate his father's swift movements but struggling with the heavy load. He looked over to the path leading to the jungle and shivered at the memory of what had happened the week before. A cow had wandered into the jungle and he was told to retrieve it. Just as he left the clearing he noticed a tiger's footprints and deep marks where another animal had been dragged along. He turned and raced home as fast as his legs could carry him.

That night one of his father's friends hid on a platform in a tree waiting for the tiger to appear. Early the next morning he returned victorious to the village and the boy recalled his own share in the adventure with some satisfaction now that it was safely over.

When at last he finished his chores Ben set out to look for his friends, but they were nowhere to be found. Finally he decided to go down to his favourite tree, a big oak with a root jutting out like the head of an elephant. It was a wonderful place to pretend and build castles in the air. He tucked himself into the curves of the root and closed his eyes. "If I could have just one wish," he thought, "what would that wish be?"

He imagined himself as a captain in the Army, leading his soldiers into battle, and being awarded a medal for bravery. Then he imagined himself as a white-coated doctor in a busy hospital, with a stethoscope round his neck. He thought of being a maharajah, with all the money he could want, with a vast palace, wonderful clothes, jewels and horses.

"I cannot be all of these things," the boy said to himself. "If I could have only one thing, what would it be?"

And at once he knew the answer:" I would want to go to heaven."

Sitting in the shade of the tree, he dared to dream of two more wishes: "I'd like to go round the world." It was a tall order for one who had never seen a bicycle, nor a bullock cart, nor a train! "I'd like to have good health all my life." As a little boy, he was plagued by sickness. Now that he was going to school, and wanted to play football, good health would be very important to him.

In the Spring of 1935, while in Class 6, he joined the Christian Endeavour Society at school. Each month new students would be selected to speak, and his turn came sooner than he expected. As he looked through the book which gave suggestions for topics, one caught his eye: "I shall be a Christian in my life's work." He decided to speak on that. But when the time came to stand before three hundred and fifty boys and girls, he hardly knew what to say! He stumbled through his talk and sat down, hot with shame. He was troubled for days afterwards, and finally it dawned on him: *How did he dare choose such a subject, when he himself was not a Christian?*

He began to rise early each morning and open the Bible. He read a few verses, then a chapter, then more, beginning to study what Jesus said and why He said it. Slowly it became clear to him that he must accept Jesus for himself. It was not enough that his father was an elder in the church and a teacher in the mission school. Even though he was brought up in a Christian home, it was just as important for him to make that decision personally as it was for his grandfather to 'cross the bamboo' those many years earlier!

As soon as he made this decision, he wanted to be baptised. But the church was twenty miles from his school. Nothing daunted, he set off at the first opportunity.

Ben returned to school knowing that he was a 'new person'. His conversion had been quiet but very meaningful. He had not been converted through a missionary's sermon or a 'revival' meeting, but simply by reading God's Word. Through it he discovered that God could speak to him personally, and so began a life-long habit of 'living by the Book'.

Ben completed his schooling and went on to St Paul's College in Calcutta. Financially it was a great struggle for his father, but Ben was an excellent student and his father wanted to keep him in college as long as he could afford to do so.

Meanwhile the world was in ferment: the Second World War had stretched its deadly fingers into the North East territories and at the same time there was an internal struggle to throw off the British yoke in India. Ben was attracted to the college groups who voiced their dedication to Indian freedom. He too became resentful of British imperialism. Outraged students gathered many stories of injustice, mismanagement or cruelty by the British 'oppressors'. Ben listened avidly to these accounts and was himself deeply disturbed.

He admired the teaching of Mahatma Gandhi, and wanted to dedicate himself to the cause of peace and freedom. Should he be a lawyer? How could he more effectively help to right the many wrongs perpetrated by the British?

But the more he pursued the ideal of peace, the more troubled he became within himself. One day in 1943 the turning point came. He found himself asking the question:

"Am I an Indian first or a Christian first?" and he realised that he was putting political issues above spiritual ones. The more he had become involved with militant groups (militantly pursuing peace!) the more restless and disturbed he had felt. He recalled how, as a boy of fourteen, he had opened his heart to Jesus Christ, and the peace of God had then invaded his life. At that time he had had no doubt about what came first!

All the conflicts, wars and protests of recent years had almost succeeded in making him forget that 'peace that passes understanding' that only Jesus could give him. Right then, he knew the answer: "I am a Christian first, and an Indian second."

After that he dedicated himself more deeply to living for Christ. His studies in college took on greater significance, and he worked even harder than previously. But one day he received disturbing news: he would have to withdraw from college. His father deeply regretted that he could no longer support Ben's studies, but it was becoming financially impossible.

Ben went along to the college principal, Mr. P. Mahanty, and told him the sad news. What he didn't realise was that a missionary by the name of Dr. J. W. Cook had been watching Ben for a long time. He knew that this was a young man being prepared by God for a special role in India's future. When Dr. Cook learnt that Ben was about to leave, he knew he must not let this happen. In fact he was already making even greater plans for him.

"India needs educated Christians," Dr. Cook told him later, "for tomorrow's leaders. You must continue your education, and I will pay for your final year at college. But after that," he went on to the surprised Ben, "I think God wants you to go to the United States for further study. I believe I am to finance you for that, too."

Late in 1949 a young Indian stood at the rail of a boat leaving the USA, watching the skyline of San Francisco recede into the distance. After four years of study and two more academic degrees, he was going home. He looked down at the silver dollar in his hand. A few days before leaving the area, he had spoken at a Baptist Church in Michigan. After the service someone had approached him and pressed the coin into his palm.

"Please take this as a seed planted for the growth of the gospel in your homeland," the stranger murmured and disappeared. Now Ben looked at the coin, and prayed: "Lord, multiply this for blessing our people through the Scriptures."

He was very keen to get the full Bible translated into the Ao Naga tongue, and eager to discuss this with Naga church leaders on his return. Of course the Assam Bible was available in the area, with both the Old and New Testaments. But he could not be satisfied while the Ao Nagas - and there were nearly one hundred thousand of them - did not have the full Scriptures in their own language. Dr. Clark had translated the New Testament in the early years of the century, but even that needed revision to bring it up to date.

Ben reflected on his four years in the States, on the blessing and provision of God and on the love of Christians like Dr. and Mrs. Cook who had been like parents to him. His time at Northern Baptist Theological Seminary, then Moody and then Wheaton, had been well spent. But he was now eager to go home to the work God had for him.

He thought of the little boy cradled in the root of the oak tree those twenty years earlier. Those child-like wishes seemed more than that now! He was indeed on his way to heaven; he had come halfway round the world; and he had enjoyed good health in the many varied climates he had visited.

Now he was too old for wishes but leaning on the railing with his face set for home he found himself praying: "Use me in any way to bring the Word of God to the Ao Nagas. You have blessed me so much during these four years; please grant that my life will be able to touch at least one person each day whether in challenging, counselling, inspiring or saving a soul."

TWENTY SIX

The silver seed grows

*Awake, O man, the bright dawn is ushered for a new day
The slumber of darkness and night are over
The rosy fingers of dawn have opened before all
The golden gates of the sun of righteousness.*

Rig Veda

Dr. Ben Wati became a teacher in the Bible College in Jorhat, then a national secretary of the Evangelical Fellowship of India. By 1961 he had become Executive Secretary, a job which took him increasingly throughout the world.

But whatever his responsibilities, which now included a wife and family, and wherever he went, he continued the task he had set himself on his return from America - the translation of the Scriptures into Ao Naga. On planes or trains, the Ao Naga Bible was his 'hand-luggage' and whenever he had a few spare moments, he would slip open the manuscript and tackle another verse or two. He grappled with the complex terms the Naga family have for family relationships; he puzzled how to translate the variety of musical instruments when the tribespeople only knew drums and flutes; he searched for ways to express colours like 'purple', because only basic colours are described in Ao Naga. Finally, in 1964, fourteen years after beginning the task, Ben completed the translation of the Old Testament in Ao, and revised the New Testament originally translated by Dr. Clark.

In 1968 Ben Wati was elected President of the World Evangelical Fellowship, the first Asian so honoured. Other distinctions followed in recognition of his leadership and translation work. But this Christian scholar and leader remained a quiet and humble man, who walked with God and prayed for India.

One day as he was praying, a vision for revival flashed

upon him. This led to an article shortly afterwards in *The Pastor's Bulletin,* of which he was editor. It was entitled: *Wanted: 100 Churches,* and asked for a chain of prayer to encompass the whole of India, with individual churches from a wide range of denominations "crying to God for mercy upon our land and upon our Church." They would continue in prayer for twenty-four hours before the prayer would be adopted by the next group in the chain. Ben wrote:

> As we look upon India's social and political situation we are compelled to pray for God's mercy. And God intends mercy upon the teeming millions. We believe this is possible only through Jesus Christ, the world's and therefore India's Saviour.

The chain started at the Gauhati Baptist Church in Assam, and Ben Wati was heartened to note university professors, doctors, nurses, students, policemen, housewives and children all taking part. The prayer chain criss-crossed the nation, with groups at Ahmedabad, Simla, Lucknow, Nagaland, Palayamkottai, Sagar, Bombay and onwards joining each other in prayer for their beloved land. Outbreaks of revival were reported in many quarters: there was a church in Orissa where one hundred and ninety-seven new Christians were baptised in one day.

Later, Ben Wati's own home territory experienced the fresh wind of the Holy Spirit rushing through the Naga Hills. It was 1972, the centenary of the planting of the Christian Church in Nagaland. A centennial Hall had been built in Impur, erected on the site of Ben Wati's birth. Thousands of Naga Christians felt the date was significant. In 1872 there were nine Christian converts in Molung village. By 1885 fifty-one Nagas were followers of Jesus Christ. Less than one hundred years later, the majority of Nagas - seven hundred thousand - subscribed to the Christian faith! Yet many evangelicals (and Ben was among them) believed that Nagaland's tribes needed to rediscover the love and forgiveness of Jesus Christ, and the power of the Holy Spirit. They wanted revival. As is often the case, eager Christians can try to turn a spark into a flame by crusades and conferences, missions and meetings. There was a flurry of activity in that direction. The evangelists came and went, but nothing happened.

Then came the rice harvest. All the able-bodied men, women and children were in the fields, and only the old and infirm remained in the village. One afternoon someone made a suggestion: "Let's have a prayer meeting in the church while the others are working."

Suddenly the Spirit of God descended upon the old people. Some described it later as like thunder, or an earthquake. The presence of God was felt as never before. But revival was first of all a great conviction of sin. People fell on their knees and faces before God repenting of the coldness of their hearts towards Him and apathy towards the lost souls who did not yet know Him. They made a rediscovery of God in all His holiness.

Someone broke away from this heavenly visitation and rushed into the rice fields. "Come quickly!" he cried. "God is blessing our church!" The men and women ran into the village, not stopping to wash or change their clothes. They hurried to the church at once.

The moment they entered they all felt the power of the presence of God. Men and women began to praise God as never before. Many began to cry aloud at the realisation of their own coldness. People began to pray for forgiveness of hidden sins, and some beat their breasts as they repented. Neighbours who had not been on speaking terms were tearfully and joyfully reconciled. It sounded like confusion and mayhem, but everyone was being dealt with in different ways. God knew what each person needed, and He was doing a special work in each one.

For forty-eight hours they stayed in that church building, neither eating nor drinking nor sleeping. Even the children and babies were quiet and not once disturbed the others when they had to leave. Some Christians lay prostrate on the floor, praying silently. Some discovered they were healed and began to testify. Some received special spiritual gifts, and signs and wonders. A village boy, deaf and dumb, was healed - and immediately went to the platform and began to praise God for it. A lame man was healed, and began to dance before the Lord!

There were hundreds of parrots in the area who would normally seize such an opportunity to swoop down on an unattended harvest. But when revival came, the Christians forgot about the birds....

The following day, neighbouring villagers from higher up looked down on the deserted rice fields and wondered what had happened. They came down the path to find out. "We could see no one working in your fields," they said. "But there wasn't a single bird there, either!"

The revival caused the people to long for more teaching. For two years they began to attend Bible studies at five o'clock each morning and again every night. Christians were making a deeper commitment of their lives to Christ, but also non-Christians in the area were drawn to the church and to Jesus. The only problem was that now people had to arrive hours before a service if they wanted a seat! And that year - as revival spread throughout Nagaland - *ten thousand people became followers of Christ and were baptised.*

Ben Wati's years of work within the Church in India increased his conviction that Indian Christians have a vital role to play in bringing blessing and prosperity to the land. He expressed his views in a talk given some years ago which was afterwards published:

> Nineteen hundred years ago, according to tradition,the gospel came to India first through St. Thomas, the doubting disciple of Jesus.
> Spiritual giants like Bishop Abraham Malpan of Kerala, Bishop Azariah of Dornakal, Sadhu Sundar Singh of the Punjab, and Pandita Ramabai of Mukti Mission near Pune have made a lasting contribution to the Church. We miss them today.

The world may not regard them highly, though a few among them could have easily filled any office it could offer. But then the economy of God has never rested on people whom the world has deemed fit. No earthly potentate, for instance, would ever think of using fishermen, slaves and tentmakers to extend the frontiers of his kingdom. This was exactly what the Lord of the Church did. How could He do it? We know the answer. Quite ordinary were the human instruments. But they were man mastered by God, the Holy Spirit, dispensing blessings wherever they went.

The Church in India, too, consists of ordinary people. We may also be a blessing to our land, but only if we yield control to the same Spirit of God. He is willing to use us for the good of the land and for the glory of God. Just one condition needs to be met. And that is, the people of God must turn their back on sin, not toying with evil in any form. Then will righteousness flow like a river in the Church. And the Church in turn will pass on its holy infection to our nation. 'Righteousness exalts a nation but sin is a reproach to any people.'*

---

* 'Whither Evangelicals' - Dr. Ben Wati, GLS Press, Bombay, c. 1975.